Cryptocurrency Investing

Beginners simple Guide to Bitcoin & other Cryptocurrency Investment

Abdullah Mamun, FCCA

Copyright © (2021) by Abdullah Mamun
All rights reserved.

In no way is it legal to reproduce, duplicate, or transmit any part of this document in either electronic means or in printed format. Recording of this publication is strictly prohibited and any storage of this document is not allowed unless with written permission from the publisher. The author owns all copyrights (surefinancialfreedom@gmail.com)

The information provided herein is stated to be truthful and consistent, in that any liability, in terms of inattention or otherwise, by any usage or abuse of any policies, processes, or directions contained within is the solitary and utter responsibility of the recipient reader. Under no circumstances will any legal responsibility or blame be held against the publisher for any reparation, damages, or monetary loss due to the information herein, either directly or indirectly.

The information herein is offered for informational purposes solely, and is universal as so. This book is not offering any financial advice specific to your situation. Before making any financial commitment, you should seek advice from qualified financial or legal practitioner. The presentation of the information is without contract or any type of guarantee assurance.

All trademarks and brands within this book are for clarifying purposes only and are the owned by the owners themselves, not affiliated with this document.

Dedication

To Musa!

My dearest darling child. I wish You will be the youngest generous crypto multi-millionaire of our family. You will be riding the wave of new era of Cryptocurrency smoothly.

Table of Contents

Introduction	5
About the Author	8
Introduction to Cryptocurrency	9
The Difference Between Traditional Fiat Money & Cryptocurrency	11
The History of Cryptocurrency	11
What Is Cryptography?	13
The Blockchain	14
The Digital Currency: Bitcoin	17
Tokens Versus Digital Coins	20
Myths About Bitcoin	21
Fundamental and Technical Analysis of Bitcoin	25
Bitcoin vs Other Cryptocurrency	28
Causes of The Fluctuations in Bitcoin Market Value?	32
Factors that Caused Major Crash in Bitcoin Price	34
Buying, Receiving and Storing Bitcoin	36
Bitcoin for future Wealth	41
Online and Offline Storage	41
The Taxation of Bitcoin	43
Create a Crypto Wealth Portfolio With low Risk	46
Building A Cryptocurrency Portfolio	46
The Investment Potentials In The Different Types Of Cryptocurrency	50
Minimizing The Risk In Cryptocurrency Portfolio	51
Make Money by Mining $1,000 a Month	53
Can You Be A Millionaire By Investing In Cryptocurrency?	57

How the Blockchain Technology Changing the World	**62**
How To Avoid Crypto Scams	**66**
How are Crypto Scammers Screwing Common People?	**66**
How To Avoid or Minimize Crypto Risks?	**69**
Conclusion	**70**
Feedback!	**71**
References	**72**

Introduction

Is Bitcoin worse than Dutch Tulip bulb market bubble?

Is it possible to make a million dollar by investing in Cryptocurrency?

Is Digital Currency really taking over traditional cash?

You might have read the news that people made millions off Bitcoin. It made you wonder why you didn't invest in Bitcoin earlier. Then you heard the news that the price fell sharply and rose again. No wonder, you don't feel confident about investing in Cryptocurrency.

Or You are confused which cryptocurrency to invest. You read few google articles to learn about Bitcoin, but still on the fence to invest in cryptocurrency. You want to make profit from investing in cryptocurrency without making a loss. Ultimately, you want to create wealth and your financial independence out of cryptocurrency investment.

This book will clear all your confusion and the most burning questions on cryptocurrency.

If you have never heard about Dogecoin, Ethereum or any Altcoins, I will have to ask you where in the world you have been. Still, this book is deliberately simplified to give you the foundational knowledge you need to invest in Bitcoin and other cryptocurrencies.

Cryptocurrency is one of the trendiest topics in the world right now, and Bitcoin is one of the top coins in this industry. Investment in cryptocurrency is one of the best and easiest ways to achieve financial independence.

There were more than 4,000 cryptocurrencies in the world as of January 2021. If you don't know the fundamentals about a particular coin that you are going to invest, chances are, you might end up losing it all.

According to Warren Buffet, the best type of investment you can make is investing in yourself. Why? The answer is simple. As your knowledge increases, especially about cryptocurrency, so does your income.

"If you don't believe it or don't get it, I don't have the time to try to convince you, sorry."
– Satoshi Nakamoto (father of Bitcoin)

The biggest Bitcoin investors are the people that were brave enough to believe in the future of digital currency. Yet, others have also made a fortune from this business. Therefore, it is not too late for you. There is no doubt that the crypto world offers endless opportunities to earn money and achieve financial freedom.

However, it is also full of volatility, which makes it possible that you lose all your money. I am not telling you this to scare you. Rather, I am highlighting the risks involved when you don't have enough information.

I know there are many people out there who need to have access to quality information that will enable them to navigate this industry without falling into some of the common pitfalls, especially beginners. It is the desire to meet this need that has inspired me to write this book. You can trust me to help you on this journey because I have been a seasoned investor in Bitcoin and other coins with great potentials. My success so far has made some people assume that I am lucky. However, you need more than a slice of good luck to be a successful cryptocurrency investor.

I have not achieved success as a cryptocurrency investor because Lady Luck smiled on me, but because of one or two things that I know about the industry. It always makes me sad when I see people trying to convince others on social media that Bitcoin isn't worth it because of their personal experience. How I wish these people learned from the right source. This book is borne out of my desire to share my knowledge with more people so that they can avoid the potential pitfalls in the industry.

This book had been written to teach you all there is to know about Bitcoin and Cryptocurrency investment in general. In this book, you will be taught from scratch the Introduction of cryptocurrency, how it works, and blockchain innovation in general.

Also, you will learn about the different terms associated with the Cryptocurrency markets, how to buy, receive, store Bitcoin, and the best ways to make money from cryptocurrencies.

You will understand why the price of bitcoin or any cryptocurrency rises and fall.

There is a dedicated chapter on fundamental and technical analysis of Bitcoin. This chapter will make you a savvy investor, you will know what to look for while investing in a cryptocurrency.

There is a step-by-step guide on buying, storing and receiving Bitcoins. Many people lost their Bitcoin as they didn't store it properly. You will learn the correct methods of saving coins.

Taxation of Bitcoin also has been discussed in simple language. You will know how much tax you need to pay in case of capital gain from cryptocurrency Investment. No surprise that many people don't know the taxation rules on Cryptocurrency investment.

Also, the easiest method to earn a million dollar potentially from Cryptocurrency investment has been discussed.

In the final chapter, how to detect crypto scams and how not to fall for any scams have been discussed.

To wrap it all up, this book contains all the information you need to be successful in the cryptocurrency market. So, you have nothing to worry about if you have little or no prior knowledge of the market.

This book doesn't provide any specific advice to invest in Bitcoin or any other cryptocurrency. Rather, it will make you knowledgeable about the Cryptocurrency investment.

About the Author

I am a professional qualified Accountant and an ex-investment banker. I worked in the fascinating world of Investing at Big Banks. Previously, I reviewed many investment proposals including Initial Coin Offering (ICO) for Cryptocurrency investment. From my experiences, I discovered fundamentals to look for while investing in a crypto coin and avoid loss. I have included all the tactics that you can learn from me in this book so that you can invest in a cryptocurrency confidently. Overall, you will understand the blockchain technology and how it is shaping our world.

All you have to do is to walk with me. Are you ready? Let's set sail!

Chapter-I
Introduction to Cryptocurrency

Success is not an accident

I. The Very Beginning; Currency Evolution

Generally, daily transactions, trade, or in simpler words - the process of giving and taking has been a part of Man since his history. The nature of the human is wired in such a way that it always seeks a return in favor of giving anything. And this very nature originated the primitive mode of payment: the Barter system.

Growing through centuries, we came to an era where trade and that "give and take process" became the essence of daily lives. The whole society and even governments were structured on this phenomenon. Consequently, a new payment mode was inevitable. Currencies, cash, precious gems, and stones became part of trade and payment structures.

Now, in the twenty-first, we live in that period where businesses and organizations are looking for fintech or contactless modes of payment. Though the story began with the coining of the term - plastic money, it has now arrived at a revolutionizing moment. At this moment, digital currency is emerging, seeking to take over the financial markets.

This contactless mode of payment is not only revolutionizing daily transactions, but it is also being considered as an additional security layer for trade and financial agreements.

II. The Birthplace of Altcoins; The Need for Alternative Payment Modes

Many factors led to the origin of alternative currencies and amongst these, financial freedom tops the list. When fiat currency faces any crisis, consumers prefer to use the alternate currency to bypass any potential barriers. The second reason for alternate currency is the advancement of technology that is constantly pushing away barriers to the ease of doing business. Thirdly and most often, the alternate currency is brought to market just to improve local business.

Lastly, economic uncertainties and speculations motivate consumers to look for alternate investment modes. And the encouraging factor here is that Alternate currencies, especially cryptocurrency, provides solutions to such investment problems.

Therefore, it is this socio-economic environment that has always urged governments and currency regulators to keep introducing alternate currencies that will be beneficial to all.

III. Examples of Digital Currencies

It is quite normal nowadays to earn tokens, coins, or points while shopping or traveling. For instance, if you are on air travel, you may get some air miles as a complementary gesture. Those air miles are examples of digital currency. To name a few, you can consider the following examples: points awarded after meal or shopping; tokens and badges earned in an online game; and tokens received for availing any similar facility. These digital currencies can also be cashed in the form of fiat currency - however, it varies from case to case.

IV. What is Cryptocurrency

Cryptocurrency is a type of digital currency. It is the electronic mode of payment where no financial institutions are required for payment transactions. Or in simpler words- you can directly send money to the recipient without seeking permission from financial institutes. Cryptocurrency provides the facility of money transactions no matter where people are located in the world in a short span.

A briefing feature of cryptocurrency is that it is not circulated by any government authority. Government has no control over transactions or withdrawal within the cryptocurrency system. It is a totally computer-based method so that people can have complete peace of mind while investing their money according to the cryptocurrency method. The decentralized, public ledger makes it easy for users to track and trace all electronic transactions. It keeps a record of transactions, thus keeping the process transparent and open.

V. The Features of Cryptocurrency

The general features of cryptocurrency primarily include decentralized peer-to-peer, and speedy transactions. Moreover, its software is open-source: authentic software developers can even make changes that are needed by the software. Third, this currency is global, secure, reliable, and flexible. Also, it can be scaled accordingly and it offers automatic integration. Through automatic integration, any relevant software can be linked with the ledger that can help in maintaining payment rules.

Success is not an accident: you need to be mindful while mapping your journey towards success. This is what Timofei! a media student did. Timofei is a Russian village dweller. He lives with his grandmother. Once he got $100 from his grandmother and thought to invest in cryptocurrency. He did so to earn money for shooting his films. Whatever he earns as profit from this investment, he uses it to shoot films. Recently, one of his films got featured in the Switzerland Film Festival and Moscow's Museum of Modern Art. Surely, this success was not accidental.

The Difference Between Traditional Fiat Money & Cryptocurrency

First, fiat money is legally approved in most countries because it is comparatively more stable than the cryptocurrency. Second, every fiat is controlled by the government of its respective country, for instance, USD is regulated by the US government. Whereas cryptocurrency is an overall computer-controlled currency without any inference from the government.

Additionally, both of these currencies are used for payments and as a store of value. However, cryptocurrency is more reliable than fiat as it is tamper-proof and can't be spent twice. Also, a cryptocurrency does not allow you to reverse or cancel your transaction. Another major difference between these two is that fiat currency, usually, is backed by a physical element -mainly gold - which is a nonrenewable or perishable resource. In contrast, cryptocurrency is not backed by any physical object. In fact, there is no intrinsic value measured for cryptocurrency. Due to technological backup, the cryptocurrency will run longer.

Moreover, cryptocurrency can be spent, received, or transferred by anyone at any place and at any time without any need of a bank or government's interference. Meanwhile, one needs to go through several steps for their international traditional fiat money transfer which is time-consuming.

Although despite these differences, cryptocurrency and fiat currency have two essential common features. They both allow smooth payment methods between two parties or marketplaces and can act as a huge store of value.

Briefly, cryptocurrency allows you to do money exchange with fiat currency around the world according to its current market value. Whereas those people who own cryptocurrency can easily make purchases from all around the world where cryptocurrency is approved legally. Besides, the people with fiat currency don't face the problem of their currency being illegal in any country.

A senior executive of a Dubai-based firm, Christopher, shared his story with Khaleej Times. He started investing in cryptocurrency after reading different success stories and being inspired by them. He invested in four cryptos. Though he observed a profitable trend, two of his cryptos are going in a loss. He shared that he has learned from his experience that you need to learn basics while jumping into the market. According to him, this currency class is more volatile and would take time to gain trust.

The History of Cryptocurrency

Cryptocurrency has been a part of human history since the day the internet was developed. The global connection motivated IT experts to remove barriers between financial transactions. This thought developed the primitive nature of cryptocurrency. Since that time, cryptocurrency has been evolving. But the breakthrough in its history came when David Chaum pitched the idea of untraceable digital cash.

I. David Chaum: Godfather of Anonymous Communications

In 1983, David Chaum proposed an idea in a magazine, Digi Cash. In that, he presented his thoughts about the anonymity of people involved in financial transactions. According to him, it is important to maintain the privacy of people involved in financial deals. Due to this, he suggested the idea of a digital currency - a currency that is difficult to trace.

In the perusal of his idea, David launched a company with the name Digi Cash. However, he had to close it in 1989 as the company was declared bankrupt.

II. The Launch of e-Gold and PayPal

Though Digi Cash went bankrupt, the idea of digital currency had convinced many minds and many experts came to find the best possible solutions. Although banks launched the technology for online payment, including Debit and Credit cards at the time, the technical faults during online transfer did not offer a smooth mechanism. Consumers had to face some restrictions due to the bank's server failure. Unfortunately, many times bank consumers still have to face similar problems. This technical failure interrupts the payment process and slows it down.

So, in the 1990s, a team of IT experts launched e-Gold to solve the aforementioned problems. E-Gold was the first digital currency mode that offered an irreversible transaction facility. The platform offered digital transfer of gold between two peers without revealing their identity. Though the website became very famous at the time and gathered around five million users, the US government had to shut it down. The reason for this shutdown was the increasing cases of cyber-crimes: the feature of user's anonymity appealed to many cyber-criminals and they started using e-Gold for criminal activities.

Later, in 1998, PayPal launched and offered a medium for peer-to-peer digital transfer of fiat money. This platform is still operational and is being used globally by more than 361 million active users (May'21). However, the difference between cryptocurrency and the PayPal technology is that the former is solely digital and is not backed by any fiat money whereas PayPal is backed by fiat currency.

III. From Bit Gold to B-money

Meanwhile, in 1997, a team from NSA, US National Security Agency, proposed a system like Bitcoin in one of its papers. Later in 1998, Nick Szabo took this concept a bit further and introduced a system called Bit Gold. This technology can be called a primitive form of Bitcoin. The goal for Nick Szabo was to cut out the role of middleman in this technology.

This technology was reformed with Wei Dai; a computer scientist's introduction of B-money; a digital currency. During his work, he suggested the primary features of a cryptocurrency.

This story of cryptocurrency is still in process. Experts are still working on the technology to make it more reliable and secure. For that, much emphasis is being given to cryptography that makes the whole process safe and secure.

What Is Cryptography?

Earlier on in history, to maintain secret conversations individuals used encryption, or in simpler words: they used code language to converse. Such secret writing is called cryptography or also ciphertext. Such text is produced in a way that only the sender and receiver can decrypt the language. Thus, it assures the secrecy of both.

Encryption helped people by converting plain text conversation into code words in the form of ciphertext. Cryptography is somewhat similar to encryption. It is a part of cryptography but not the whole. It is a process that keeps information secure by changing the plain text into algorithms and mathematical operations. That way, only the intended recipients can read the message.

From King Caesar to Queen Mary and then Nazi's Enigma, history is filled with the importance of cryptography. King Caesar was said to be the first person to introduce secret language. Later on, in World War II, a secret language-producing typewriter, Enigma, played a vital role. However, these early forms of cryptography were physical.

With the advancement in computers, cryptography was taken to the level of software. In 1977, NSA and IBM jointly introduced a Data Encryption Standard (DES). However, till 1999, many computers were able to decrypt the DES easily, hence leaving a question on the capability and purpose of DES. To counter this issue, Advanced Encryption Standard (AES) was proposed in 2001. This is the success of AES that to date, it is being widely used as the most secure cryptographic language.

AES securely transfers data from sender to recipient and requires users on both ends to use a key. Thus, through AES, that key is delivered securely even within a public network. However, it depends upon the type of cryptography the way that key is exchanged.

Types Of Cryptography

The three main types of cryptography are symmetric key, public key, and hash functions. All of these types play a different role in the field of cryptography.

Symmetric Key Cryptography

This cryptography consists of a secret key. As ciphering takes place, the key is set between sender and receiver. That key deciphers the text and makes it understandable to the reader. So, it is necessary to keep the key a secret. Or else, anyone can read the confidential information.

Public Key Cryptography

This type considers various methods and keys to transmit the information. Senders and receivers use multiple keys to cipher and decipher the message. Thus, each of those individuals keeps the secret key to themselves while they use the public key to regulate the information across the network.

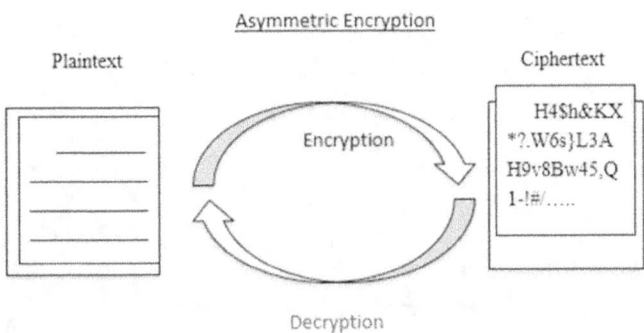

Hash Function

The hash function takes into account the arbitrary length of the message for input. Whereas, the output is an algorithm that delivers the fixed length. Experts also state it as a mathematical equation due to the reason that it demands the numerical values for input to come up with a hash message. The hash function algorithm is used by many companies worldwide to retain the privacy of their clients. For instance, Facebook has implemented SHA-algorithm system to secure their users' passwords. This system stores the hash of a user's password so every time a user logs in to their Facebook account, Facebook calculates the hash of *this* password, compares it with the original hash and if the two hashes match, the user successfully logs in, and can access their account. In case of a single mistake, the hash will not match and the access to the account will be denied.

The Blockchain

To make the process of digital transactions secure and tamper-free, many techniques were proposed. One technique was about record keeping of these transactions. Therefore, in 1991, a digital ledger was developed, called a blockchain.

Blockchain, as the name suggests, are blocks of data or information transferred during digital transactions. They are like digital timestamps which are impossible to backdate. A blockchain is open publicly. This is a modern way to secure the recorded information in such a way that no one can change it or hack it. Sources state that it is known as the digital ledger of transactions distributed over several computer systems. Each time a transaction adds to the record, it appears in the participant's ledger. So, the copy of the ledger is available to all the participants which make it transparent.

Furthermore, this method of securing the transaction involves a cryptographic signature that is known as the hash. The hash is helpful in several ways which include the prevention of change and reversibility. In easier words, a blockchain has three faces:

- a data face that contains data like receiver and sender's name and transaction amount.
- a hash that is a unique identity of each blockchain, just like your fingerprints
- a previous hash face, which contains the identity of the previous blockchain.

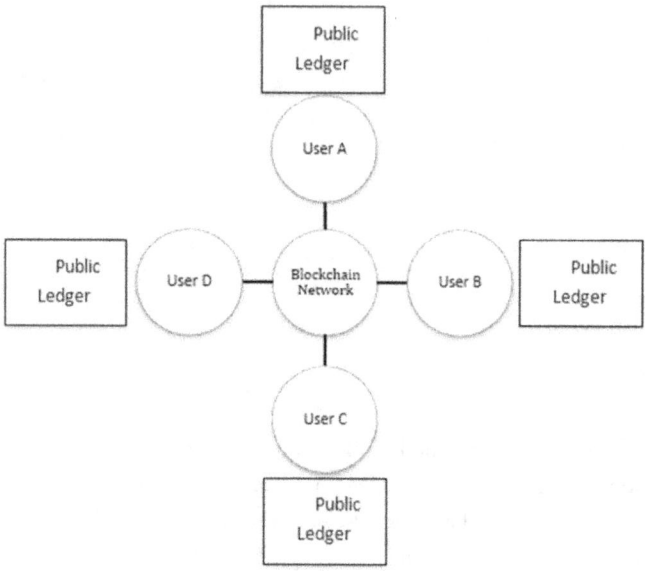

The Working of Blockchain

Now, let us consider the example of three friends: Ann, Marlin, and Joe.

Ann transferred 2 BTC to Marlin. Now during this transaction, a blockchain will be made at Ann's end with data, hash, and previous hash faces. At the data face, that blockchain would have Ann & Marlin's information and the amount. That blockchain would have a unique hash. During the transaction, that blockchain will transfer information to an adjacent one and this process will be repeated at Marlin's end too.

However, during this, if someone tries to temper the process, changes will be made in the hash that will consequently be registered in the neighboring blockchain. This way tempering is made impossible.

Blockchain technology works by the method of decentralization. This process is controlled by numerous computers. In the blockchain, a huge number of servers are connected but not on a single platform, there's a big geological computer making it a vast connection yet specifying it. During digital transactions, plenty of data is controlled by a group of people or even by individuals sitting afar. But collectively, all the computers form a chain that is called a Node.

A node contains all the basic to the latest information added in the last. Bitcoin transactions are particularly saved in the Data. So, if the data of a single node gets corrupt, the other nodes will be notified. Hence, it is secure and not easily changeable.

Let's recall that example. As the network is completely open, anyone can join it. Now Joe wants to be part of the chain. He will get a full copy of the blockchain and the node will verify it. After a few times, Joe sent 3 BTC to Ann, hence a new block would be formed. This block would be sent to the three of them - Joe, Ann, and Marlin. At this moment, each node would verify this block to know whether it is tempered with or not. After verification, that block would be added to the blockchain by each node. This way, every node in this network needs to have a consensus about the authentication of that block.

If anyone plans to bring an unwanted change in the blockchain, it will be easily noted as the other chains highlight it. Thus, it is a transparent matter.

Regarding the change, the several computers/ users need to agree on a particular change. This goes to show how the majority becomes an authority. And this is in the best interest of people.

How Does Blockchain Ensure Transparency?

There are different ways to ensure transparency in bitcoin transactions. To view transaction details, you can either form a single page to view the changes, or open a link. The document and link, just like a statement of account for traditional transactions show transactions and details about the lows and highs of Bitcoin. While it is possible for Bitcoins to be stolen, stolen altcoins can be tracked and retrieved using this medium.

These three principles also help to validate the transparency, and security of bitcoin transaction,

- The first of these principles is hinged on the unique identity of each block in the form of its hash. If it is altered, the subsequent block will invalidate the process.
- The second has to do with the proof-of-work: every block requires ten minutes to calculate the proof-of-work of its previous block. So, in case the process is interrupted during any block by a hacker, he would have to invest ten minutes on each block to recalculate their proof-of-work.
- Lastly, for the purpose of transparency, Bitcoin transaction by default is kept open to everyone and uses a peer-to-peer protocol.

So whenever a change is added, the hash changes too. That is a plus point in the security of the process. If a hacker intends to steal Bitcoin and he changes the code bar (hash) of a single node, other users will suspect and can even cross-check as the changed hash will stand out among all other nodes.

For a successful hacking process, the hacker needs a high hand by covering at least 51% of the blockchain information. This is the standing rule to bring a mass change that is not highlighted. And it is really tough and even difficult as this process has been made highly expensive. Changing the blocks and even the change of hash bars are pretty expensive.

In essence, with all of these requirements, the process of tempering with the blockchain is mostly always futile. Every drastic change will never go unnoticed. They always catch the attention of users. And the moment foul play is detected on the block chain, users begin to opt for safer platforms and hence decreases the amount of the previous Bitcoin, thereby making it useless. So, it is safer to be included in the trade and gain from its benefits than to attack it.

The Digital Currency: Bitcoin

Whenever people talk about Bitcoin ratings and demand, it gets interesting and enticing. You can hardly resist the urge to invest. But in the real sense, it is essential to know what Bitcoin is and how it works before getting into investment full-fledged. So, let's get into the introduction of what Bitcoin is to better understand subsequent chapters.

In 2009 Bitcoin, which is currently the most influential currency was invented. The major motive behind the creation of this currency was to build trust among users and provide a decentralized system for users from all over the world. Bitcoin is a computer-based currency that is stored in digital wallets and can be sent and received from using safe and secure online platforms.

When any user performs a Bitcoin transaction, this transaction is recorded in the blockchain. And nowadays, various online and offline exchange forums are operated to help users with fast transaction and currency conversion issues.

The main motive of inventing the cryptocurrency system is to provide privacy and safety to user's assets. This virtual currency is to provide a convenient payment system that takes out the involvement of intermediate or middleman institutions.

The Bitcoin Ecosystem

As technology advances, risks and fraud issues also increase. The Bitcoin ecosystem is built on the structures of technological advancement and operates in such a way that it facilitates user autonomy and secures their assets without control or charges from a central body. Using crypto protocols, this currency protects users from criminal activities. The Bitcoin ecosystem, encourages businesspersons, investors, and users to trade and interact using digital channels and platforms. Miners and traders are the major components of the Bitcoin ecosystem.

Other components of this ecosystem include merchants, consumers, and hoarders.

- Miners are the primary producers in the Bitcoin ecosystem: they mine or receive Bitcoin.
- Traders try to maintain the cycle. They convert Bitcoin to fiat and back. The aim of traders is to make profit from the sales and purchase of Bitcoin when the coins hit a greater value.

- Merchants are players who receive payments for services in the form of Bitcoin. They are registered business outlets or institutions that have Bitcoin listed as a mean of payment for their goods or services.
- Hoarders are players who buy Bitcoins, hold it over a period, and eventually sell when coins have increased in value. They save Bitcoin just to make a profit at the event that the prices shoot up. According to Ron & Shamir, around 55% to 73% of Bitcoin are being kept by hoarders. (Ron & Shamir, 2012, p. 10)
- Consumers are people who use Bitcoin as a means of settlement of debt or means of payment for goods bought or sold. Thus, they do not look for profits of any sort neither do they consider the coins for investment purposes. They just use Bitcoin as a mode of payment.

Activities of Miners and Bitcoin Mining

Miners play a very vital role in securing daily Bitcoin transactions and ensuring that they are scam-free. Mining is a computer process that operates within the transaction with the aim of verifying Bitcoin transactions. It is the authentication process that results in merging the transaction data with the Bitcoin ledger along with past transaction information data.

So, in simpler terms, miners resolve computational problems and hence get Bitcoin in the form of reward. So, they earn money without necessarily spending money. Eventually, these verified blocks later become part of the blockchain. So, to earn bitcoin, you either buy or mine. Mining is however a tougher route. Miners are requested to solve complex puzzles or network problems before earning. Purchasing, which is the simpler option involves you buying Bitcoin from exchange platforms to either trade or hold.

Note that, Bitcoin is neither mined like gold nor printed on paper like fiat currency. It does not have any of these physical properties. It is likened to gold in that it is just like other nonrenewable resource, and is also finite. The truth is that only 21 million Bitcoins are available to be mined and in just over ten years, 18.6 million Bitcoin have already been mined. (That was as at Jan 2021). The balance of 2.3 million will be mined in 120 years. This is as a result of the Bitcoin halving. The number of Bitcoin that has been produced per block is now cut in half in every four years. In 2024, the mining reward will drop from 6.25 BTC per block to 3.125 BTC per block.

Now that you understand the periodic halving of Bitcoin, the question therefore is: "what will happen once all the 21 million Bitcoin are mined? How would miners be rewarded?

Well, once Bitcoin has reached full mining potential, mining will no longer be rewarded with block rewards but with transaction fees.

So, here is an explainer example on how a miner mines Bitcoin:

Joe is interested in mining Bitcoin. He has a computer and spends some time daily solving the mathematical algorithms through which he mines Bitcoin. He also verifies Bitcoin transactions and tries to prevent fraud. So, he is now being compensated for his hard work in the form of Bitcoin. That is how he mines Bitcoin. So, he is being paid twice: one for verifying the transactions; second for mining the Bitcoin.

This profitable mining lures many to jump into this hurdle. However, the process of mining is getting competitive day by day. This strict environment was once proposed by Satoshi Nakamoto as he knew that many people would be attracted to mining. Therefore, he wanted to increase difficulty in the mining process with the arrival of several miners.

You might be surprised that miners are highly paid. This is because they have to verify each transaction and, secure the transaction thereby preventing hackers and the activities of users who use digital currency illegally. The motive behind mining transactions is to ensure loyalty among the Bitcoin users and run a smooth way for Bitcoin transactions. Moreover, miners save users from double-spending issues where users can spend the same Bitcoin two times.

How Does Double Spending Occur?

In the case of fiat cash, the issue of double spending is nonexistent as you need to hand the money over in exchange for a product, service or the order of both. So, in actual fact for fiat, after placing an order or spending any amount of cash, you do not have that same amount. However, in the case of digital or virtual currency users might use the same Bitcoin twice and thus affect the security concerns of blockchain.

Another way to deliberately double spend is by getting the photocopy of the user can make a copy of the original. Spend its copy while retaining the original Bitcoin. Here miners perform their role by verifying transactions that are worth around 1MB or they have to generate a random hexadecimal number to verify the transactions. This guesswork or creation of hexadecimal numbers is not an easy task and the user has to go through lengthy steps. However, it does not involve any sort of complex mathematical queries. Some people have the opinion that Bitcoin mining is like a huge lottery because miners have to compete with other members of th4e network. Using their hardware, they have to generate a unique hash number. The faster your hardware you can perform the more tries and hence the chances of your victory enhance accordingly.

The purpose of Bitcoin mining and the reward pave way for users to earn and purchase Bitcoin. Thus, encouraging people to invest in cryptocurrencies and expand their businesses.

Currently Using cryptocurrencies?

According to recent statistics report, over 4,000 cryptocurrencies were in existence in January 2021. With this information, I consider it alarming that only 20 cryptocurrencies occupy the top where about 90% of the market meets.

In fact, not all of them are in usage, some of them are in less or no use. Some of these currencies are as follows

Bitcoin(BTC), Ethereum (ETH), Ripple/XRP(XRP), Litecoin (LTC), Binance coin (BNB), Tether(USDT), Cardano (ADA), Bitcoin SV(BSV), Bitcoin Cash(BCH), Dogecoin, and many more. However among the most using and well-known cryptocurrencies are Bitcoin, Ethereum, Dogecoin, Ripple(XRP), Bitcoin cash, Litecoin.

Tokens Versus Digital Coins

A digital coin is a digital asset that is generated as a part of its blockchain. In further explanation, coins operate on their blockchains. As an example; Bitcoin functions and operates on its blockchain, whereas Ether operates on its blockchain and it is the same for Litecoin. These coins work a bit differently from fiat cash coins. In this case the user can store coins, can transfer them or can place them in wallets to use in the future. As an example:

You can use Bitcoin to transfer money, to perform any transaction and you can save Bitcoin to use it later.

On the other hand, tokens are such digital current it's that you use for transferring an asset that has physical existence. For instance, you want to transfer property paper over an open network through digital information, you will use a token. So, they represent something that has physical value, whereas digital coins have only digital or virtual information.

Tokens are produced on an already existing blockchain. Majorly the tokens that are commonly used are created on the Ethereum platform. The tokens that are produced are referred to as ERC tokens. Various other platforms are also working to create tokens like NEO, List, Waves, and others. As Ethereum tokens are ERC-20, similarly NEO tokens are NEP-5 tokens. The developers or programmers can use these tokens in their applications to activate various features of their applications.

Briefly to conclude the overwhelming effect of cryptocurrency has resolved many time and security issues. Yet the user must be conscious about the platforms and exchange forums while performing transactions. Providing invalid details or even a little mistake can cause the loss of your Bitcoin.

Thanks to technology that has created safe zones for storing virtual currency. Yes, you can keep your assets safe in digital wallets that are operated under blockchain technology. These wallets are also available online and free of cost in variety. These are numerous based on their functions. Users can get their wallet each of which has a unique address to immune your digital asset.

You can navigate to know the best and reliable platforms where you can download hard wallets or soft wallets or as per your need. Former is used to store money offline, preventing access from anywhere except stakeholders. Whereas, soft wallets allow storing money online so users can do transactions also when required. The purpose of both of them to provide security else your asset would be vulnerable to cyber or hacking attacks.

Chapter-II
Myths About Bitcoin

"Sometimes, myths lead us to the way of truth"

The rise & progress and demand for Bitcoin are indisputable. No one can deny that since its creation, there has been an exponential rise in the demand for bitcoin in the market, since their creation. Previously people considered that all the news were rumors and myths. However, with time and awareness, people realized the necessity for secure cryptocurrency.

The aim behind the invention of digital currency is to provide a scam-free, secure, and decentralized financial system. In this chapter, we will reflect on the myths on Bitcoin; burst the myths and discuss how one can earn money and gain profit either via trading or investing in Bitcoin. These myths are similar to other cryptocurrencies.

Myths about Bitcoin

Since Bitcoin's creation until now everyone accepts the phenomenal success of Bitcoin. Whether you are a Bitcoin holder or you are a Bitcoin opponent, still, everyone believes that Bitcoin has come a long way. The myths in this read will help you to clarify the facts and these are not the rumors.

Fraudulent Scheme

Still, today, few people believe that Bitcoin is a fraudulent scheme and as such avoid investing in Bitcoin. Later on, as soon as some prominent other companies like Tesla invested in Bitcoin and started accepted Bitcoin payment, then people shifted their thinking about virtual currency and started investing in this breakthrough technology. However, the use of digital currency has made money transactions easy and now people do not have to wait for so long to do international transactions. Moreover, users can transfer Bitcoin from anywhere to anywhere.

A money-making scheme

Another major misconception about Bitcoin is that it is a bubble that is meant to fascinate the greed of people. Previously people did not believe in this digital currency. instead, they started criticizing the rise in the price of Bitcoin. However, when people saw that Bitcoin price hit more than $100, their opinion about the altcoin changed. Presently, business owners and individuals alike purchase items ranging in sizes of big to small items from Amazon or any other shopping center. The number of Bitcoin ATMs is now on the increase. You can readily convert cryptocurrency to traditional cash seamlessly and almost immediately. This goes to show how deep the influence that Bitcoin now has on the public.

Safety and Security Concerns

Cryptocurrency is not considered to be safe regarding security and safety concerns. Because of the possibility of hackers and scammers attacking the exchange forums, investors and traders are confused about trading in digital currency. Over time, blockchain has proven itself to be free from any of such activity and that its security is tight enough to protect the digital assets. Now users can more securely protect their digital currency in wallets to immune cryptocurrency and can use it for a long time.

Is Crypto a Good Alternative for Money?

Have you thought about traveling to a new country? Do you worry about visiting different currency exchange platforms? Escape all those hectic processes by investing in cryptocurrency, with secured electric currency. Have you thought about the need for digital currencies? The question is since there is fiat cash all around the world, with each country having its different currency why then is there the need for a digital currency?

Well, digital or virtual currency is just like the replacement of fiat cash with another's country currency.

While inventing cryptocurrency, the developers and stockholders declared their intention to introduce a new way to protect your asset and gain more profit shortly. Currently, it is considered wise to keep at least 10 Bitcoin instead of having $100. Why?

Because of the way the price of cryptocurrency, especially Bitcoin is increasing, it presently ranks as number one. The analysis sometimes calls it the gold of the future. Even now, the Bitcoin millionaire advised the younger generation to invest at least 10% of their income in cryptocurrency.

With time, you never know how much its price will increase, and then you will realize how much profit you have gained.

Thus, to conclude, it is better to invest and trade in cryptocurrency before it is too late because the rapid graph of its price has a minimum chance for lowering its price. The economy of a country may be at the loss but the price of Bitcoin keeps on increasing as its demand remains on a hike. It will not be surprising to hear the rise in Bitcoin price around $100,000. The main reason is due to inclusion of major investors and companies in cryptocurrency.

Is Bitcoin A Bubble?

As the millennials investing in crypto, the price of Bitcoin grows within the generation and this prompts the same criticism that has plagued the digital currency system for the past decade. As the price of Bitcoin stayed on the increase, it earned the nominal clause 'bubble'. Moreover, research shows that any kind of fiat or digital money that isn't backed up by a commodity just as gold or silver can be considered a bubble. However, economists on the other hand are proven to be bad at detecting or modeling these kinds of bubbles.

Furthermore, the study explains that the cause of growing Bitcoin is more likely to be one of these two factors: the momentum and the amount of exposure that a Bitcoin receives. This means that if Bitcoin has gone up more than a normal range then on an average it will continuously keep going up. Also, studies have revealed that in the current situation, the bubble is more likely to be triggered by over-optimism of the technologies that are considered to still perform a major role in the future but the researchers do not find it worth paying the prize that people are now paying for them at the peak of their enthusiasm.

Briefly, calling Bitcoin a bubble carries two major drawbacks. There is this cyclical existence of Bitcoin prize which clarifies that a standard bubble never stays any longer, it pops and then vanishes. The bubble does not continue to be a bubble indefinitely. A commodity has to be trading for much longer than the value of the asset underneath the Bitcoin for a bubble to occur. For anything like a Bitcoin, this is much more difficult to assess, however, according to the study, it can be worth a shot but the marketplaces carry a different point of view about the Bitcoin bubble issue due to its demand.

Why Is Bitcoin Considered the King of Crypto?

There's no doubt that Bitcoin is the blockchain industry's forerunner; which is one of the biggest benefits at least in retrospect. It is the very first accepted digital currency. The first Bitcoin was mined in the year 2009. No other currency appeared until 2011. The companies that came after Bitcoin had to scramble for attention as thousands of people had been using it already and also it was mined by a thousand more.

Additionally, at that time a single Bitcoin was only rated around thirteen dollars, although that changed. Research shows that more than eight million Bitcoin were roaming in the market before the second crypto came into existence, it is incredibly holding fifty percent market shares now. This means that half of the virtual currencies are Bitcoin and what else can be the proof for Bitcoin being the king of cryptocurrencies?

Most importantly, Bitcoin has become a legitimate form of payment among numerous online stores, even in physical stores. Celebrities, tech experts like Elon Musk, Bill Gates, Winklevoss Twins, Ashton Kutcher highly invested in Bitcoin and speaks in media about it.

Moreover, investing in Bitcoin for retirement purposes can bring in considerably high returns and will diversify your portfolio. Yet one thing that is proven by studies about cryptocurrencies is that they are incredibly unpredictable and very risky. Also, digital currencies have grown in popularity as a savings medium to the point that they can now be held in several individual retirement accounts and help to facilitate people during retirement as well. Additionally, by investing in Bitcoin, people can have a great opportunity to compare it with the best technology investments and choose the best for themselves.

Chapter-III
Fundamental and Technical Analysis of Bitcoin

The Ups and downs make business lively

Fundamentals Of Bitcoin - Its Technology and Networks

Back in 2008, when Bitcoin was invented as a cryptocurrency, individuals assumed it would close down soon, as such, only few people showed interest in investment in the coin. However, in the world of digital or internet currency, things are quite unpredictable. So, Bitcoin's value started rising. Currently there are 51 million to 54 million active traders in the world

As cryptocurrency doesn't have any mechanism to discount future cashflow and determine its value like a stock, it is hard to measure the real value of a cryptocurrency.

Its payment method operates on a cryptographic protocol. Besides, Bitcoin is a decentralized currency that people buy and sell using a public distributed ledger known as the blockchain. It records the transactions regarding Bitcoin and other cryptocurrencies worldwide.

The main driver of a cryptocurrency price is the demand and supply mechanism.

As new transactions are made, a set of information makes up a block. These blocks join together to form a blockchain. Once the hash and nodes are included, it makes the process transparent and makes the transactions viewable to every user. Also, if someone tries to edit or hack, the hash code changes in the blockchain which makes it detectable easily.

Market Capitalization of Bitcoin

Individuals often inquire about the worth of anything before investing any amount in it. The same goes for Bitcoin. The market capitalization assures if Bitcoin is dominant in the market or not.

Discussing Bitcoin's market capitalization, it rose to 400 billion US Dollars in January 2021, with comparisons to the summer months. At the moment, it is more than 600 billion US Dollars. Starting from 2013, it had the worth of one million US Dollars in the market. However, the way Bitcoin earned popularity in 2017 changed everything.

The process of calculating the market capitalization demands multiplying the Bitcoin's total number in motion by the price of Bitcoin. As the rising popularity is spreading more awareness about Bitcoin, several websites have come to existence that demonstrates the market capitalization of all cryptocurrencies. One of them is Coinmarketcap which is the most popular market capitalization website currently.

The Market Cap of Other Major Coins

Other than Bitcoin, there are several major coins of the cryptocurrency that play a great role in the cryptosystem. However, none is as dominant as Bitcoin in the market. The first dominant major coin after Bitcoin is the Ethereum. It is the first time that it reached 138 billion US Dollars in January 2021. Whereas, last year in August 2020, it was not even half of that worth.

Next is the Litecoin. It reached the market capitalization of 10.1 billion US Dollars by January 2021. This success made it the sixth-largest cryptocurrency in the world. Cardano's worth is just a bit lesser than Litecoin with a market capitalization of 9.8 billion US Dollars.

Another is the unique proof-of-stake cryptocurrency known by the name of Polkadot. January 2021 set its market capitalization of 11.2 billion US Dollars. The coin with the least market capitalization among the discussed cryptocurrencies up till now is Stellar. As it has a market capitalization of 6.1 billion US Dollars. Tether is known to have a smooth fluctuating process compared to other cryptocurrencies that fluctuate rapidly. Thus, its market capitalization was set at 24.4 billion US Dollars in the January of 2021.

While doing the technical analysis, it is worth mentioning some few other points.

The Hash Rate

Before hopping on to the hash rate, it is significant to know about Bitcoin mining. Bitcoin mining is a process in which the workers verify the legitimacy of the transactions. By doing so, they prevent the issue of double-spending for the users. Thus, the cryptographers use the hash rates to render the information of a Bitcoin transaction by forming a blockchain.

In short, the hash rate is one of the metrics that indicates the hard work of miners. As the miners use this to compute and validate the blockchain of Bitcoin. The more power (hash rate) they consume, the more secure it becomes. Thus, a larger hash rate denotes attractive mining. Also, it leads towards a better outlook for Bitcoin's price in the future.

Although Bitcoin is an internet currency, it still needs to be mined by solving complicated mathematics computations. When an individual does a Bitcoin transaction, it forms a blockchain. The hash rates make the transaction blocks permanent in the ledger.

Bitcoin Halving

Block mining is infinite; it does not end as transactions are continuous. The block reward is halved after each set of 210,000 blocks is mined, roughly after four years. The reward that Bitcoin miners get for processing the transactions is cut in a half. The half-rate is the rate at which a new Bitcoin is introduced and it circulates afterwards.

Sources state that this process would continue till the year 2140. And at that time, the users will pay a fee for mining and miners would get this fee as a reward for processing the transactions. This assures that miners' work is not taken for granted and the network will keep working like that. Inquiring about the significance of halving takes an individual to an answer that marks a drop in Bitcoin's supply. Thus, embarking upon the total maximum supply of Bitcoin, it is 21 million.

The most recent Bitcoin halving took place on the 11th of May, 2020. Before that, it happened in 2012, and at the time, the Bitcoin halving rate was 25. After that, it became 12.5, and recently in May 2020, the Bitcoin halving rate became 6.25 BTC for each block. However, there are many halving complications. One of them is the reduced supply of Bitcoin with every halving. So, less supply gives birth to more demands, and it consequently raises the price of a Bitcoin.

Bitcoin's Traders

Bitcoin traders are players who run the exchange platforms that enhance user's cryptocurrency purchase or spending and in return, earn huge profits.

Their main focus is to regulate the circulation of Bitcoin and cash currency to engage people. With time, as the trend and use for Bitcoin or any cryptocurrency increases, their price also increases. Suppose, merchants at shopping malls start accepting Bitcoin as a payment method, this would result in a rapid increase in the price of BTCs.

The Demand and Supply of Bitcoin

The price of Bitcoin abates and touches the sky depending on two factors; the demand and supply. So, it is significant that you know about it. If the supply decreases, demand and prices increase. Whereas, more supply leads to moderate demand and low price of a Bitcoin. Unlike fiat money, Bitcoin comes in a limited supply which is why investors have been buying a large number of Bitcoin, thereby the demand for Bitcoin is touching the sky.

The supply crisis is affecting the market massively. The total number of mined blocks has been increasing rapidly due to transactions. These circumstances have made it harder for the new investors to buy Bitcoin as the unit price of Bitcoin has increased. Besides, the researchers and expert traders have predicted and assumed that prices will go higher in the upcoming months as the supply of Bitcoin does not look like it will get stable anytime soon.

The Implication of Investing in Large Capitalized Cryptocurrency

When investing in cryptocurrencies, individuals think that a large capitalization is beneficial. Instead of looking forward to the current rates of cryptocurrencies, it is good to seek the indicators. Market capitalization is one of those indicators bit not all that there is to consider. When any currency has set a large capitalization, it denotes that there are a good number of investors who stick by that currency and do transactions.

One of its greatest examples is Bitcoin and Ethereum. These have set a large capitalization till now. So, it is safe to invest in these cryptocurrencies. Note that cryptocurrencies with a market cap of ten billion or more are considered large-cap currencies and good to invest in. Whereas, if the market cap is between 2 billion and 10 billion, the currencies are mid cap. However, the riskiest investments are in companies with a market cap of 300 million to 2 million.

Thus, the more large-cap the currency, the more stable it is to invest in it as there is less price fluctuations. Additionally, the investments and a large number of transactions denote their good quality and stability.

Bitcoin vs Other Cryptocurrency

Although Bitcoin takes the lead in the competition among cryptocurrencies. One other major player in the industry is Ethereum. Bitcoin and Ethereum have many similarities. For instance, both currencies use blockchain technology and have the highest market capitalization. Additionally, both of the currencies are decentralized and are not in control of any bank or government. However, there are some distinctions.

Languages

Ethereum runs its language; Ether on the network. While Bitcoin facilitates the users in various aspects as it can be an alternative to national currencies and also the medium of exchange. Whereas, Ethereum facilitates smart contracts and decentralized applications through its currency. However, Ethereum supports the blockchain and indirectly supports the Bitcoin network. The popularity it has earned has pushed it between the other cryptocurrencies for the competition.

As various cryptocurrencies are entering the market, the public interest is fluctuating. Other than Bitcoin and Ethereum, Litecoin is also in the competition. It is a non-Bitcoin crypto that has managed to participate in the competition by standing at the sixth number after Bitcoin. The area that significantly demonstrates the differences between Bitcoin and Litecoin is the market capitalization and dollar market value in total.

However, Litecoin is distinguished from Bitcoin with its accommodation of 84 million coins. Meanwhile, Bitcoin accommodates up to 21 million coins only. The other impressive crypto for the current year has been Stellar. There are many differences between Bitcoin and Stellar. The most highlighted is the consensus protocol.

Stellar's consensus protocol does not rely on the miners to legitimate the transactions. Instead, it goes for the FBA algorithm that renders the processing of transactions.

Dogecoin

Dogecoin began as a joke, but no one is laughing anymore. It was an elaborate prank that went too far. It is a form of digital money, just like Bitcoin. It runs on peer-to-peer transactions across a decentralized network. The explosion of the Dogecoin subreddit brought about mining pools and services, which are the infrastructure any coin needs to become successful. It gained popularity quickly, and it has been on the rise since.

Bitcoin Versus Dogecoin

There are many similarities between Bitcoin and Dogecoin. However, they are not the same. Due to the changes Dogecoin miners made in the ecosystem, they are usually called "diggers" instead of "miners." Also, instead of relying on the SHA-256 consensus mechanism, which Bitcoin uses to secure its network, it relies on scrypt technology within its Proof-of-Work (PoW) mechanism. Dogecoin also reduced block times in comparison to Bitcoin.

Investing In Small Capitalization Crypto

When any trader invests in small-cap crypto, we say that the trader has invested in the currency with a low market capitalization. It is risky as the chances of failure are at the peak. Additionally, those currencies have not reached their full potential. Therefore, investment might lead to high-level risks and even losses.

Although it is riskier, many investors invest in them and witness a successful portfolio. It depends on the affordability of the risk to be able to tell if the investor will be able to bear it or not. While it is risky, it is not outrightly bad. So, to invest here, traders must consider many important factors.

However, small-cap coins have the potential to grow. Hence, they are beneficial. So for this reason, they might eventually pay off. Remember that Bitcoin was once a small capitalization crypto. But, you need to focus on the market to take the risk. Also, it is important to make yourself available on various platforms and websites so that you can always stay updated on news about the cryptosystem. As these coins have low cost and are easy to trade, anyone can cause fluctuation in their price by simply trading some coins. Therefore, it offers greater growth potential.

Institutional Investment That Drives the Price

The demand for Bitcoin is increasing rapidly and the reason is not farfetched. The growth is due to the activities of investors like the city of Miami and Tesla. Recently these institutions announced plans to invest in Bitcoin and with this, people assumed that prices would go high.

So, when Tesla announced his intention to invest 1.5 billion dollars from its balance sheet, the Bitcoin's price went to $48,000 dollars. Thus, institutional investors are looking forward to the benefits they can get from Bitcoin and other cryptocurrencies. Moreover, Uber's CEO and PayPal demonstrate that they are setting the Bitcoin as a potential means of payment therefore increasing the need to buy and trade in the currency.

Companies Considering Investment in Bitcoin

With every increase in bitcoin investment prospects, a new case comes up. Truth be told, the desire to invest in a digital currency might seem a little absurd to the audience at the moment but Bitcoin is the future, which is why S&P 500 other companies are considering investing in Bitcoin. Recently, the CEO of MicroStrategy revealed about adding more to the reservation of Bitcoin. Besides, the step has triggered such a domino that might influence other companies to invest in Bitcoin as well.

Moreover, the CEO of Twitter and Square who is a great Bitcoin champion stated that the internet's native currency would eventually become Bitcoin. The Pomp Podcast's Saylor even revealed that his half-board owns Bitcoin.

In September, the talks about investing in Bitcoin skyrocketed, the investors believed that the S&P 500 companies will eventually possess Bitcoin on their balance sheets by the end of the year 2021.

However, the results of the survey regarding this revealed that 44 participants stated that 5 to 9 companies would buy Bitcoin, sixteen sounded optimistic as made a list of ten companies to buy bitcoin and the rest of the participants stated that there would be fewer companies holding Bitcoin at the end of the year 2021. Now, everyone is looking forward to the end of the year 2021 as it would clear the doubts of many participants and critics.

S&P 500 Companies Considering Investment in Bitcoin

The S&P 500 is a financial exchange benchmark that covers five hundred large-cap companies in the United States. It reflects the stock market's success by monitoring the risks and returns of the topmost companies. Also, investors use the stock benchmark of these companies against which all other transactions are measured.

Furthermore, according to the blockchains' annual outlook report analysts already expect that S&P 500 constituent firms are more likely to have Bitcoin on their balance sheets as soon as possible, according to 51.4 percent of the 44 survey participants. Also, about sixteen percent predicted positively that ten or more businesses would carry Bitcoin.

Moreover, if any company from the S&P companies invests one percent of their money in Bitcoin, the price will rise around forty thousand dollars. Ark estimated that if a company from the

S&P 500 companies is investing ten percent of their money in Bitcoin then the blockchain is more likely to rise around four hundred thousand dollars.

The US States that Approved Bitcoin

Blockchain is merely a method for handling databases of mining or cryptocurrencies. The State governments in the United States also recognize the potentials of the technology and its ability to improve the quality of public services, and hence are in varying phases of deployment. In 2014, the Mayor of California signed a bill that ensured the legality of "various forms of alternative currency such as digital currency" in transacting payments and purchase of goods, hence making California one of the first states to conform to the biddings of the operation of crypto regulation and control. Many famous cryptocurrencies such as Coinbase, Kraken, and Ripple also have their headquarters located in California.

Accordingly, two American states also adopted legislative actions that are directed at the crypto space on the 14th of August 2020. The first was Maryland's attorney general who confirmed the space participation in the operation crypto sweep, which was a collaborative effort between provincial and state security authorities in the U.S and Canada.

On the other hand, Nevada announced new conditions for crypto ATM operators, requiring them to obtain a transmission certificate. For the first location issued by the license, business owners are more likely to pay the maximum range of ten thousand dollars. Also, an additional five thousand dollars is needed for each additional kiosk.

USA Cryptosystem Policy Especially towards China and Iran led to a Higher Price

China has quietly drafted an economic and security partnership with Iran leading to even more conflicts with the US. The question therefore is that will this silent US/China conflict ever end? Well, we will never know. However, this rocky political climate has sickened the public and apprehension is now on the rise. Moreover, due to the growing popularity of Bitcoin, many countries have also recognized the importance of the digital nature of the currency which is why many countries including China are now developing their own national digital currency.

China, however, is one step ahead of most countries even the US, as it has already developed a national currency called digital yuan. Yuan is now being used in limited geographical locations in its trial period.

This is slowly turning into a contest. So, while the idea of investing in a decentralized currency has always seemed ideal to the citizens, now more than ever, the US citizens are more than willing to invest in a digital and decentralized currency of value, unlike the US dollars that is prone to the risk of inflation.

This digital currency will never run into risk of inflation during wars or even more conflicts. This is true due to the fact that Bitcoin is wholly independent and strictly limited. This limited supply has increased the demand of the currency, attracting citizen who can foresee the inevitable conflicts or wars between the countries in the future and can predict the higher demand of digital currency in future.

Causes of The Fluctuations in Bitcoin Market Value?

The growth Curves

Bitcoin's price experiences fluctuations a lot because it is presently only in its early stages of growth. The legality of Bitcoin has been the subject of much discussion and speculation. The average person is newly learning about Bitcoin and considering investment. Just as Bitcoin price fell from twelve hundred dollars to four hundred dollars after MtGox was hacked in 2011.

Distributed Denial of Service (DDoS)

Another major reason is in crypto jacking. The growing popularity of Bitcoin has attracted crypto jacking in the form of Distributed Denial of Service (DDoS) attacks by cybercriminals and hackers. These DDoS attacks have triggered a six to ten percent drop in Bitcoin price. Also, internal strife over the scaling problem is ragging. The two parties in the Bitcoin creation world disagreeing on the path Bitcoin is more likely to follow in the future. This has a major impact on Bitcoin's scalability and valuation.

The nature of the currency

Additionally, Bitcoin is also used in illegal activities, different kinds of scams and schemes. And the truth is that occurrences like this is more likely to have a huge negative impact on the Bitcoin price. But this cancels out when an average person who is learning about Bitcoin invests in it. This can be a cause of definite increase in the value of Bitcoin, especially when this is done in large scale all around the world.

Other factors

Janet Yellen, the US treasury secretary released the warning about the threat that Bitcoin presents to both investors and the general public. Also, due to support from a variety of outlets the cryptocurrency was still trading above fifty-three thousand dollars after the steep drop in price to start it over again. Briefly, the Bitcoin price is affected by fresh Bitcoin growth or bad press. People have experienced it drop by thirty percent in a week and grow by thirty percent in the same week mainly due to news and speculation.

The Power of the US Government's Printing Money!

The Federal Government's ability to make and annihilate money is what gives it so much power. People are concerned with the federal reserve printing money while simultaneously wholly unaware of the fact that the Federal Government is capable of 'unprinting' the money as well, meaning that money can easily disappear in thin air this is due to the power the Federal Government holds.

To minimize liquidity, the Federal Government only needs to employ contractionary monetary policies; which is the same as withdrawing money from circulation. The Federal Government raises the federal funds rate to limit the volume of cash in the money supply. As a result, the bank is more likely to have less cash to lend.

The Federal Reserve is also capable of influencing interest rates, including credit cards, mortgages, and bank loans. This is done by the federal funds rate; the interest rate banks pay for overnight borrowing in the federal funds market. It also influences the value of the U.S. dollar in the market and can both, directly and indirectly cause inflation of money.

Moreover, when the federal funds rate rises, all interest rates rise with them. Loaning money for business growth, cars or housings becomes more expensive. And this, as a result stifles the economic growth and thereby, suffocates the market that fuels inflation. Additionally, quantitative easing may also be withdrawn by the Federal Government. This is accomplished by issuing treasury bonds and mortgage-backed securities to financial institutions.

People are concerned that banks will refuse to purchase these shares, however, they have no alternatives available rather than moving along with it. Furthermore, Federal government's capability to generate and kill wealth can monetize the US debt.

It is important that you do not confuse the U.S. Treasury for the Federal Reserve as they both are separate units serving different purposes. The Treasury manages all of the money coming into the government as well as the money paid out by it. Meanwhile, the Federal Reserve on the other hand has the responsibility to keep the economy stable by managing the supply of money in circulation.

Interestingly, one of the customers of the Treasury is the federal reserve itself. However, treasuries are kept on the balance sheet. In theory that the treasury would repay federal reserve at some stage. Until then, the federal reserve increases the amount of the funding available to the federal government. Also, the federal reserve replaces dollars on banks and balance sheets with these shares, which clarifies the cause of people worrying about the US government printing money.

Why Do People Think the Dollar Is Fake Money, And Prefer Bitcoin?

Due to Bitcoin's distinguishing characteristics and its solid foundations, Bitcoin is more valued than any kind of fiat money. Also, it is valuable because of its rarity which is why plenty of people purchase it on exchanges like Coinbase, Primex Bt, and Kraken. It is also seen as a shield against bad monetary policies with the central bank printing currency at unprecedented rates.

Bitcoin continues to keep getting more value because it performs admirably in six areas that are scarcity, divisibility, utility, portability, longevity, and counterfeit ability. Whereas no fiat currency can carry all of these qualities that Bitcoin facilitates to any person, anywhere across the globe.

Since Bitcoin comes in a limited supply, it has fought off any risk of inflation. It is known to be the best performing investment of the last nine years. Additionally, it is a profitable brand that is reasonably difficult to purchase. However, there are many perks to investing in Bitcoins. It is a currency that comes with a guarantee of a lifetime which can be invested in whatever business an individual might desire.

In several ways, Bitcoin resembles gold while USD will merely be written, that's the reason why people think that dollar is fake money because after getting unlimited facilities from Bitcoin, USD has no value left as compared to Bitcoin.

The Hype Created by Media About Bitcoin

Cryptocurrencies are now generating a lot of buzz in the industry. A few years earlier, we only just knew about the developer of Bitcoin. But nowadays, all the media in the world publishes news about it. Social media has turned our world into a global village and news, undeniably, spreads like a wildfire in this village.

So, something as astounding as cryptocurrency has caught the attention of millions on social media which has to lead its popularity and fame in recent years. People have undoubtedly seen each and every one debating about it and exchanging crypto news. So it is safe to say that Bitcoin and other cryptocurrencies owe the credits of their fame to the active and curious social media users.

Factors that Caused Major Crash in Bitcoin Price

Even the most seasoned economists have been puzzled by Bitcoin's rapid price volatility, particularly when its price fluctuations are barely correlated with any other currency, asset, or value store traded on the global markets. Bitcoin has continually been a victim of rise and fall of currency. This disaster is affected by a number of aspects.

Buyers and sellers on Bitcoin exchanges are the people that determine the price of Bitcoin. Buyers want to pay low prices while sellers want to be paid the highest. Additionally, margin trading the bitcoin currency also causes a fluctuation in the price almost 90% of the time that results in even more losses and bringing the price down.

Moreover, media has also played its part in plummeting price of Bitcoin in the market. The negative press of media has declared Bitcoin as a dead currency more than 350 times over the past few years, causing extreme distress and panic among the public and potential investors, leading to potential investors to back out of their investments. These two, among many others, are the reasons why Bitcoins has faces so many crashes in the market

Bitcoin's power usage:

In February 2021, Elon Musk publicly mentioned that Tesla purchased $1.5 billion of Bitcoin and will accept the cryptocurrency as future means of payments from the customers. This news created a massive surge in Bitcoin price from $39,000 to $65,000 in April. Fast forward a few short weeks, He again announced that Tesla sold 10% of its Bitcoin stake.

Because of the escalating use of fossil fuels i.e. coal for Bitcoin Mining and transactions, Elon musk won't accept Bitcoin. This made the Bitcoin price nosedive to $45,000.

Bill Gates doesn't like the fact that it uses more electricity than the electricity consumption of a small country. Bitcoin's carbon footprint is equivalent to New Zealand of 37 MT CO_2e.

Now, let's look at other platforms Carbon footprint.

- Amazon, Netflix- 100 MT CO_2e
- Porn Sites Data Centre- 80MT CO_2e
- YouTube data Centre- 64MT CO_2e
- Email Service- 620 MT CO_2e

So, you can see it's not only the bitcoin but our digital world is leaving more carbon footprint on the planet. I do agree with Elon that more clean energy should be used. Recently, he announced that Tesla would accept Bitcoin again if Bitcoin miners use 50% clean energy. However, future Bitcoin prices won't be dependent on his tweets.

Chapter-IV
Buying, Receiving and Storing Bitcoin

Learning keeps you alive

How To Buy Bitcoin - On Coinbase Using Bank Account?

Coinbase has proven to be the biggest Bitcoin exchange and broker across the globe. People can buy and sell deals to other users on the site using their exchange; known as Coinbase pro while Coinbase takes a share of the transaction. Moreover, people do purchase cryptocurrency from Coinbase at the price they offer for the brokerage with no bidding on the brokerage side.

Additionally, despite keeping a huge number of customer funds that hackers would love to grab, Coinbase has never experienced this kind of incident. This clarifies that Coinbase does an outstanding job of keeping customer funds secure on the website. Coinbase is so effective at avoiding attacks that it can also protect its customers from scams that occur outside of the network. You can only deposit to Coinbase using a debit card, credit card, PayPal and bank transfer. Among these, debit card and bank transfer are the two most common payment options for Coinbase customers.

The Process of Purchasing Bitcoin on Coinbase Using Bank Account

To buy Bitcoin on Coinbase, using the bank account first requires you to log into your Coinbase account. Afterwards, you will be required to register for an account if you don't already have one. This would include a bunch of personal details from you such as your name, email address, phone number, and so on. After you have entered all of your details, make sure to read and approve the registration terms before proceeding.

Moving forward, when you are done with the Coinbase account registration process, log in to your account. After you are logged in to your account, go to settings, click the linked accounts that will take you to a screen where bank logos are displayed. Now your job is to simply provide the bank account details of your account that you would prefer to link to it. Once you are done with this process, your bank account will be automatically be linked, allowing you to finally buy and sell screen, and purchase Bitcoin with just a click of a button.

Is Using a Bank Account Good?

If you need money but don't own a bank account, you can get a cash advance from an ATM using your credit card. You will be paid a withdrawal fee as well as interest from the credit card provider. Also, you can get free cash from your own bank's ATM whether you carry a bank account and an ATM or credit card. Although you can get your money from any ATM, If you use your bank's ATM. If you use any other debit ATM you will have to pay a transaction fee.

Since banks prefer current clients, especially those who handle their money well, banks and credit unions are more likely to assist you in obtaining credit for a house, a vehicle, a student loan, or a personal loan. Furthermore, turning to small loan providers who lend you money a little faster can be costly due to lending costs and high interest rates.

However, bank accounts are preferable over cashers and piggy banks. Also, you should note that banks charge a fee as well but not as much as credit unions, for example, if you use your debit card at an ATM that is not owned by your bank then you are more likely to be charged by it. Although it is dependent on the sort of account you have. You must however hold a certain minimum bank balance to prevent being paid. This clarifies that bank accounts are more likely to be a good choice as compared to credit unions that can be a cause of charging higher amounts from people.

The Offline Method of Storing a Coin

The most secure way to deposit Bitcoin is through an online wallet, this helps you in moving funds in and out of the wallet, as well as converting Bitcoin to other currencies like Ethereum, Dogecoin, and Litecoin. However, cold storage that holds your Bitcoin offline and away from any internet connection, is the safest choice.

Moreover, using paper and a printer is the best way to store the Bitcoin offline to store Bitcoin. First off, you need to go to the Bitaddress.org website or the Bitcoin.com paper wallet. Afterward, save the website as an HTML website file to your machine. After that, close the tab and turn off the internet connection of your computer. Eventually when you are done with that, move forward and open the Bitaddress.org or Bitcoin.com paper wallet that you saved locally.

Furthermore, to build a new Bitcoin address, follow the instructions on that website. Next, print the page until you have a pair of keys or QR codes. Also, for added protection, make sure your printer is not linked to the internet. Finally, now you can store Bitcoin from another online wallet using the latest public address or QR code.

The Online Method of Storing a Coin

Hardware wallets are security-hardened systems for storing the user's private keys in a secure hardware device. This hardware wallet has the ability to generate wallet keys and sign transactions. This system uses a seed which is stored in the internal storage of a hardware wallet, and it is normally designed to be efficiently resistant to both physical and digital attacks. This is done by signing the transaction internally and keeping the data safe and away from even the computer it has used to sign the transaction. This is an effective way to ensure the safety of data and private keys of the user.

Also, it never shares any confidential information with the computers it attaches to. Moreover, the user can spend coins easily without running any risk by using any untrustworthy device, because the private keys are isolated from any insecure environment. Hardware wallets prove to be one of the easiest ways to store Bitcoin online and are relatively user-friendly.

What Is a Bitcoin Private Key?

A Bitcoin private key is essentially a big secret number that unlocks and allows it to be sent. Each private key generates a one-of-a-kind signature that authorizes Bitcoin transactions for the user. It's called private for a purpose because it is intended to be private and not shared with anyone.

What Is a Bitcoin Public Key?

Another big number is known as a public key, which enables Bitcoin to be locked and obtained. It's called a public key eventually because it's supposed to be shared with the public and helps you in collecting money.

Now the concept of public and private key might seem a little complicated but let's take an example. You have a padlock and only you have the key that can unlock the padlock. You send this over to your friend, who write a secret message to you. Put the secret message inside a box and lock the box using the padlock that you sent.

Now, no one, not even your friend, will be able to unlock the padlock as you are the only owner of the key. The *encryption* or *public* key is a padlock which can be locked by anyone while *decryption* and *private* key is like the padlock key that only you own.

Likewise, a public key is just like an email address. People can transfer money to you through that email address. However, you're the only one with a private key or password to access the mails.

Examples Of Public and Private Key

Alice needs to be sent an encrypted email by bob. Bob eventually does this by encrypting his address to Alice by using Alice's public key, then after Alice receives the letter, she makes use of her private key, which is only in her knowledge, to decode Bob's message.

Attackers will most probably try to get into the server and read the message, but they are more likely going to fail in their mission as they lack the private key needed to decode it. Since Alice is the only person who has access to the secret key number, she would be the only one willing to decode the code. When Alice needs to reply, she will simply repeat the procedure, by the use of Bob's public key to encrypt her letter.

The Different Kinds of Wallets for Crypto

A wallet is nothing more than a mixture of your private key and public address, wallets can be classified in a bunch of worth recommended categories based on how and where they are held. Let's start with the most basic and commonly used kind of crypto wallet.

- Mobile wallets are the most used wallets in the market for Bitcoin and altcoins at the moment, owing to their portability with ease of usage. Since they are still linked to the internet and can be hacked by the developer community, mobile wallets prove to be the fourth most convenient place to store your cryptocurrencies.
- Desktop wallets for Bitcoin and other cryptocurrencies are software packages that can be installed on most desktop operating systems, including Mac, Windows, and Linux. Desktop wallets are known to be the third safest place to keep your cryptocurrencies.
- This form of the crypto wallet is recommended for long-term investors. Hardware wallets are, in particular, the most stable form of cryptocurrencies available. Hardware wallets, as the name implies, are physical machines designed to store private keys and public addresses. Finally, they are, without a doubt, the best place to store cryptocurrencies.

An Account of the Worst Bitcoin Loses Ever

While bitcoin has been a victim of cybercrime, there have been instances where bitcoins have also been reportedly disappeared into thin air due to many reasons such as loss of access to private or public key, etc. The Times report claims that as much as 20 percent of all Bitcoin, amounting for as much as $130 billion in 'real' or fiat money, is stuck in such crypto wallets with forgotten passwords that may never be recovered again. This is one of the few cons of Bitcoins.

One such famous misfortune happened to Stefan Thomas; a German programmer based in San Francisco. According to a report in New York Times, Stefan lost the password to hid digital wallet containing 7,002 Bitcoins back in 2011 which is now worth $245 million. Thomas stored all of his Bitcoin keys in Iron Key; an encrypted hard drive. The hard drive only allows 10 attempts to unlock. In case none of the password matches, the user will lose access to the hard drive - and bitcoins - forever. Unfortunately, Thomas now has only 2 attempts left to recover his wallet. Later it was confirmed that Stefan lost the paper where wrote the Iron Key password.

James Howells, an IT worker in Welsh, has a similar heart-breaking story. He in 2013 unintentionally threw 7,500 Bitcoin in a landfill. The value of those coins would have been more than a quarter-billion-dollar today. James lost his fortune as he scrapped the hard drive containing the Bitcoin private keys into a rubbish bin. This bin was later dumped at Newport, South Wales leaving no chance to get those coins back.

This indicates only disadvantage of the decentralized system of Bitcoin and blockchain technology. This system entirely restricts any intrusion or involvement from a third-party to recover the password so in events of a user losing access to their password, it will unfortunately, never be recovered and the bitcoins will be lost forever.

It's hardly been four years, yet early Bitcoin shareholders, who invested their money in crypto exchange companies might eventually be getting their money back at long last. The Japan-based cryptocurrency exchange, which processed seventy percent of all Bitcoin trades, declared bankruptcy at one point in 2014 after it was revealed that hackers had stolen eight lac and fifty thousand Bitcoin.

The loot was estimated at five hundred million dollars at that time. It has become worth five billion dollars now. The initiation of civil recovery hearings has been authorized by a Tokyo district court. Mt.Gox was the biggest loss and hurt most of the users, but as the value of the Bitcoin has dropped, plenty more people have lost large sums of money.

One more tale of cautionary tales of the Bitcoin loss is emerged by Derek Rose an Australian writer is that Rose cashes out his seventy thousand dollars savings plan in 2017 and invested it entirely in cryptocurrencies. Things were going swimmingly at first. Cryptocurrencies were surging in value, and Rose took out a loan to boost his holdings.

He was investing thousand dollars in interest per day, but he was profiting half a million dollars per day. His assets had grown to seven million dollars at one point. He responded that he wanted to buy a sports team or a yacht instead when a friend suggested he cash in. He kept using leverage and ended up losing everything.

Chapter-V
Bitcoin for future Wealth

The investment gives your future a hope

Researchers and developers while highlighting the importance of digital currency, cover the security concerns too. Although exchange forums allow safe and timely crypto to cash conversion, yet the assets on these forums are vulnerable to cyber-attacks and hackers. Let's have an insight into the foremost concepts regarding the privacy and security concerns of BTCs. Here you will learn about how to store Bitcoin online and offline.

Online and Offline Storage

Online storage of Bitcoin is referred to as containing cryptocurrency using internet access. As the name depicts with the help of the internet users can store digital assets. The concept of paper wallets or e-wallets was introduced to ensure the Bitcoin's users hostage. Navigate to authorized sites to register your digital wallet.

Everything has pros and cons, using an online wallet, one can transfer Bitcoin easily but they can be accessed by hackers.

On the other hand, offline storage is considered more reliable because here you do not need to access the internet. Users can save their Bitcoin in USB for a long time.

Digital wallets come with one public and one private keys. The public key is used to provide when you have to receive BTC or you have to send BTCs. however, you need to protect the private or primary key. Cold wallets allow users to install wallets after disconnecting the internet. Thus, ensuring complete protection of digital currencies.

The Implication of forgetting Wallet Password?

The main motive of this currency is to guarantee safety and loyalty. It is mandatory to create a strong password of around 16 characters. But it is the weakness in human nature to forget things. So let's say you have to store your Bitcoin in a hard wallet or cold wallet and when you are going to send or receive the BTCs you forget the password.

Here come limitation and verification issues, as generally, some applications allow trial chances for entering passwords. But BTC wallets won't allow this more than ten times. Because once you guess more than ten times unsuccessfully, your Bitcoin will vanish in the thin air, it is just like burned ashes. Even the service providers won't help you to refund the Bitcoin.

You may have heard the story of the guy who had about $220million Bitcoin stored in his hard wallet but forgot the private key. To avoid your loss in case of forgetting, you have to be patient. You can try one of the three mentioned possibilities:

- Must remember your password and log in details.
- Use your recovery code, a phrase of 12 words, provided to you while wallet generation. This phrase helps in generating all the keys whether private or public.
- Use password crackers

The last option is to keep your heart big as time is the best teacher and healer.

Before approaching the password crackers make sure to read their demands and privacy concerns. These are fast automated programs that are used to crack wallet passwords. But at least you have an idea about the starting of the password.

It has been estimated that these crackers have about 3,000 trillion combinations. Thus your assistance can help you to retrieve the password at the earliest possible time.

Yet another option is to use a secure password manager. This software allows users to generate secure passwords side by side and facilitates users in retrieving Bitcoin when needed. These utilities produce a cryptographically secure key for users to enhance protection levels and meet the demands of users.

Using secure wallets users can send and receive BTCs too. Using the sender option users can send or receive Bitcoin to a particular destination. Moreover, many applications nowadays are working for smooth BTC transactions and transfers.

Autonomous and steadfast applications and exchange forums have been developed where users can liquify crypto to cash. Without spending many fee charges users can convert crypto to cash and get their hands on the required cash currency.

Hence the bottom line is, whether you need to store Bitcoin for a long time or for transaction purposes prefer to use digital wallets for storing BTCs. although there are pros and cons of using wallets, however, it is not secure to keep BTCs on exchange forums. They are vulnerable to hacking attacks or cyber scams. Navigate to the authorized sites and choose the wallet category that matches your concerns and needs.

Chapter-VI
The Taxation of Bitcoin

Taxation with legislation fights against inflation

Taxation Of Bitcoin

With the evolution of cryptocurrency, Bitcoin has been successful in establishing its value in the digital world. Like every other currency in the world, Bitcoin are now considered to be a part of the taxation system worldwide. As the taxation rules differ in various parts of the world, one must have full awareness about the rules and regulations of taxation in his respective country.

Treating Bitcoin as A Property

A USA-based taxation authority, the Internal Revenue Service (IRS) declared in its recent statement that Bitcoin trading would be viewed as a property business. This means that trading the cryptocurrency for sales or exchange will have tax implications worldwide.

How to sell Self Owned Bitcoin to a third Party?

The first scenario enlists a Bitcoin investor who mined the Bitcoin using his resources. Later on, one sells the Bitcoin to a third party or exchanges the Bitcoin to buy goods for trading. When such individuals sell the Bitcoin, it creates a loop for taxation of Bitcoin.

The amount a seller collects from the third party is termed as business income in the taxation system. This sort of income is finalized after deducting the expenses encountered in the mining process.

How to Sell Bitcoin After Purchase?

The second scenario depicts an individual selling Bitcoin which is not mined by himself. Such people buy a good amount of Bitcoin from someone else and later on they sell them for a better price. On the other hand, one can also use Bitcoin bought from another person to invest in goods and services.

Such usage of Bitcoin makes them more like an asset for an investor. Likewise, a person can also exchange his Bitcoin for the equivalent price of goods. Such gain of income makes the investor eligible for capital gains in the taxation system.

Capital Gain In Bitcoin Taxation

A capital gain is a term used for the profits a person makes after selling his land, property, business, goods, stocks, or anything which he owned for a while. The value of this taxable income depends upon how long the sold-out subject was held on by the person himself before selling.

If a person sells the Bitcoin which were held by him for less than twelve months then this is termed as Short-Term Capital Gains. Tax applied in such cases would be equivalent to a normal income tax on any individual.

On the other hand, if the person sells the Bitcoin after holding them for more than a year then this binds him to pay Long Term Capital Gains for his Bitcoin.

Taxes On Bitcoin

First and foremost, you need to have access to tools for your Bitcoin. These tools consist of a trustworthy Bitcoin wallet to make your transaction safe and secure. Altogether, one will be able to calculate all the losses and gains of taxation with the help of Bitcoin tools.

The next very important step is to keep a record of every Bitcoin transaction. You can again make use of your Bitcoin wallet to ensure that your data is secured for later use. You should also measure all the capital gains by using a convenient strategy for it.

Bitcoin Taxation Over the Globe

In Australia

In Australia, there are government-owned authority named as ATO responsible for the check and balance of the taxation system. The Australian Taxation Office applied the same rules as in the United States of America on the Bitcoin taxation. Individuals residing in Australia need to pay capital gains or income taxes for their Bitcoin trading. For instance, if you're working as a cryptocurrency trader, you'll be taxed as a sole trader. After 12 months - or the end of the year - you'll tally your income and your expenses which will have a detailed record including the difference between the value of your portfolio at the beginning and end of the year – and the profits will be added to your overall taxable income.

In case, you're running an officially registered crypto business that deals in trading, mining and other crypto-related activities then you'll pay the Australian company tax rate of 27.5% instead

In Canada

The digital currency in Canada is subjected to the Income Tax Act. CRA which is Canada Revenue Agency termed the tax on Bitcoin as Barter Transaction. Any transaction which is made between two individuals without using a legal currency is known as a Barter transaction. Hence, a person living in Canada has to pay taxation for Bitcoin accordingly. The rate of taxation depends on the fact if your activity with cryptocurrency is considered a business or not. If it is considered a business then 100% of business income is taxable, whereas only 50% of capital gains are taxable. This is advantageous to the state because at the end of the day, Bitcoin is a currency of value. This value is now exceeding the value of fiat money, so the taxation only adds more value to it.

In The United Kingdom

According to Her Majesty's Revenue and Customs (HMRC), Bitcoin are termed as tokens in the United Kingdom. There can be exchange tokens, utility tokens, or security tokens. Capital Gain Tax will be applied for using Bitcoin as a personal investment. On the other hand, using Bitcoin as a part of your business will attract the Income Taxation rules of the UK. The taxation depends on two factors; If you are a higher or additional rate taxpayer, you'll have to pay a 20% capital gains tax rate and on the other hand, if you are a basic rate taxpayer then your tax rate will depend on your taxable income and the size of the gain after deduction of the allowances.

In The United States of America

In the USA, the Internal Revenue Service has named Bitcoin as a convertible virtual currency since its value is equivalent to the real currency. This rule by the IRS is subject to the implementation of the Bitcoin taxation system. This includes both long and short-term capital gains as well as the income tax rules in the USA.

Some people took this initiative as bad news for the cryptocurrency market. The Bitcoin taxation system laid down by the IRS enables the investors to be certain about their taxes. Hence, this helps them to improve their Bitcoin transactions by stepping up their tax process.

The cryptocurrency tax rate is same as capital gains tax rate. For short term capital gain, the tax rate could be between 10%-37% but for long term capital gains, you could pay as much as 0-20% of your gains. However, this depends on a few factors such as the accounting method that is used for calculating gains, the time frame you held the coins before selling (Holding period), and your overall annual income along with your tax filing status.

Chapter-VII
Create a Crypto Wealth Portfolio with Low Risk

Know your competitors before jumping on the battlefield

Being a part of the digital currency market, one should be familiar with the pros and cons of cryptocurrency. Cryptocurrency comes with a lot of ups and downs in today's world. One can never predict the profits and loss linked with your Bitcoin trading.

Therefore, it becomes mandatory for every Bitcoin user to build a reliable cryptocurrency portfolio for future investments. There's no need to wonder about the cryptocurrency portfolio. It is just like a normal portfolio you create for job opportunities worldwide. Hence, everyone can get benefits by building a Crypto Wealth portfolio.

Building A Cryptocurrency Portfolio

A cryptocurrency portfolio management is a record-keeping software that allows the users keep a detailed track of all of their cryptocurrency assets, investments and the trades. The portfolio helps you to analyze each coin's performance on every level of investment.

To create an impressive cryptocurrency portfolio, a beginner needs to have all the knowledge about the cryptocurrency market. This requires good quality research and thorough analysis about every type of coin in the digital market.

Next important thing is to create a portfolio that displays the diversity of the cryptocurrency market. This means that your cryptocurrency portfolio should have a high, medium, and low market coin. This enables the Bitcoin user to invest in different varieties of coins without facing too much risk in the future.

The last step to look for building a Cryptocurrency portfolio is to see which coin is evolving around your country. News in your country plays a huge role in determining the prices of cryptocurrency market. So before investing money in cryptocurrency, it would be a clever way to become familiar with the new trends of cryptocurrency in your country as well as in the global media.

The Types Of Cryptocurrency In The Market

Among the topmost notable coins, Bitcoin are leading the boards of cryptocurrency. However, you must consider the other coins as well while creating the cryptocurrency portfolio. This includes a variety of digital currency which makes your position in the cryptocurrency market stable.

Although Bitcoin is still a number one priority over the globe. There are several alternatives as well. Therefore, it is better not to be dependent on Bitcoin. There are other smart options to invest in the digital market as well.

Alternative Cryptocurrency Coins (Altcoins)

Altcoins refers to Alternative to Bitcoin which was created in 2011. This group of cryptocurrencies refers to any digital currency except Bitcoin. Altcoin includes:

-Namecoin

-Peercoin

-Litecoin

-Dogecoin

- Auroracoin

Other stable Altcoin includes:

Litecoin

Litecoin was introduced in the cryptocurrency world by Charlie lee in 2011. It works similarly to Bitcoin but with more improvements towards the transaction process.

Litecoin relies upon a different network which is an open-source payment system. This coin uses scripts as coding for the network.

This coin was declared as silver to Bitcoin gold due to the similarities between them. However, Litecoin makes transactions much faster and requires fewer fees than Bitcoin. According to the statistics, Litecoin is marked as the sixth largest cryptocurrency in Jan 2021.

Dogecoin (DOGE)

The code of Dogecoin and Litecoin are similar. With the similar aim of low processing fee and transaction time, Dogecoin placed in the top ten cryptocurrencies in the world. Dogecoin had a market valuation of $54 billion dollars (June 2021). From an investment perspective, I don't like the fact that 10,000 new coins are programmed and issued every minute until forever. It will create more supply than demand.

So, the price might not rise like Bitcoin. Surprisingly, its price rose steadily in 2021. It's no surprise that Elon Musk's tweets contributed to the higher price trend of Dogecoin.

Ethereum (ETH)

The second alternative to Bitcoin is Ethereum which is more like an application store for digital currency. It includes all the applications to make digital trading convenient for every user. It works as a decentralized software platform that allows various applications to run with total legacy.

The check and balance of ethereal benefits the users to be safe from any kind of fraud in the digital market. This cryptocurrency was established to provide a platform to run digital trading with no discrimination in any aspect of life. In this way, Ethereum has driven its way in the countries with less banking infrastructure and economic growth.

The network of Ethereum works with the help of tokens that are specific for each platform. Such a token has been named Ether. Ether, launched in 2015 works as a messenger on the Ethereum platform. It is now widely used by developers and investors to create and invest in trading respectively.

Despite certain limitations in the transactions, Ethereum has been able to secure the second position in the digital currency market worldwide.

Ripple (XRP)

The third type of cryptocurrency is Ripple which uses a coin named XRP as its coin. It is more like a technology that promotes cryptocurrency trading and transactions in the favor of users. It was launched by Chris Larsen and Jed McCaleb in 2012.

XRP acts as a bridge between two different currencies for exchange purposes. Ripple uses XRP through a process similar to the SWIFT network for its transactions worldwide. It consists of a group of servers through which the transactions are completed in a short time.

Bitcoin Cash (BCH)

In the history of cryptocurrency, there have always been arguments between developers and miners. Such debates lead to a settlement termed as forks. Bitcoin Cash (BCH) is the most popular hard fork in the digital market.

BCH established its roots in August 2017 as a result of the broken cryptocurrency. Splitting of digital currency results due to disagreements between different fractions. The fork consists of a new code just like a birth of a newer version of the coin.

The circumstances which led to the development of Bitcoin Cash are about the limits on the size of blocks. Bitcoin allowed one megabyte (MB). So, BCH was created to increase the size of the block from 1 MB to 8 Mbs. This resulted in a greater number of transactions being made within less time.

Comparison Between Bitcoin And Other Cryptocurrency

Bitcoin vs Ethereum

Counting down the difference between Ethereum and Bitcoin, one of the major ones includes the block time. Ether transactions take seconds for confirmation while Bitcoin require minutes to be completed. On the other hand, Algorithms used between are also very different. Ether takes help from that while Bitcoin uses SHA-256.

The other important difference is about their networks. Bitcoin is a cryptocurrency as a whole while Ethereum was created as a platform to benefit different decentralized applications to run properly. So overall, Ethereum is counted as a cryptocurrency but it is more like a way to facilitate the applications in the cryptocurrency world.

The market cap of Bitcoin is 10 times more than $147 billion while Ethereum has a market cap under $16 billion.

Bitcoin vs. Litecoin

The main difference between Bitcoin and Litecoin is seen in their market capitalization. Bitcoin has a 70 times larger market cap than Litecoin. The second difference between Bitcoin and Litecoin is the number of coins that can be produced in total. Bitcoin can produce 21 million coins while Litecoin can make up to 84 million coins.

The next thing which makes Bitcoin different from Bitcoin is block time. The block time for Litecoin is 2.5 minutes while Bitcoin is 9 minutes. Likewise, algorithms are also differencing between them. Bitcoin uses SHA-256 and Litecoin comprises scripts. Moreover, the transaction speed has proven to be advantageous for Litecoin users.

Bitcoin vs XRP

Now comes the comparison between Ripple and Bitcoin. Ripple uses XRP as a coin to work as a currency exchanger both domestically and internationally. While Bitcoin is a cryptocurrency created to facilitate business investments worldwide without third-party involvement.

Moreover, Ripple provides cheaper and faster ways of transactions while Bitcoin mainly focuses on means of decentralization. Transactions also differ between ripple and Bitcoin. Ripple takes seconds for confirmation while Bitcoin requires ten minutes for transactions.

Lastly, the market cap of Ripple (XRP) is around $13.4 billion. On the other hand, $217.9 billion is the estimated market cap of Bitcoin.

The Investment Potentials in The Different Types of Cryptocurrencies

Ethereum (ETH)

Among the popular ones, Ethereum (ETH) is known for its diversity towards blockchain. While Bitcoin serves as a topmost cryptocurrency, ETH has been able to establish its name in the digital world. Due to the worldwide trading platform, brokerage account network acceptability, ETH is considered to be a liquid asset.

As Ethereum allows multiple investment options, it is a smarter way for a beginner to start cryptocurrency trading. Moreover, Ether as a token moves towards a stronger point always. Most importantly, Ethereum's inflation plan is more transparent. Unlike traditional government, ETH has a solid plan to mitigate the risks.

Litecoin (LTC)

The second option for an investor is Litecoin which is cheaper and convenient to handle for an investor. Litecoin requires less energy and gives better outcomes than Bitcoin. Likewise, it enables the user to send transactions with four times faster speed than Bitcoin. This makes peer-to-peer networking more sustainable with Litecoins.

Litecoins are ideal for an investor who is new in the cryptocurrency world. This is because Bitcoin feasibility saves the user from extra hurdles and risks which are on the other hand always present with the Bitcoin users.

Ripple (XRP)

There are mainly three reasons for you when deciding investing in Ripple (XRP). The first one is the transaction protocol attached to the Ripple network. Ripple uses an old way of transferring money where the money is never handed directly between the sender and the recipient. It is done through an agent from both sides. So, this makes Ripple a better way of transferring money for goods and services to different areas of the world.

Secondly, Ripple has already made its position among top 15, it makes the coin super stable. Third, banks like ripple technology to send and receive money. It has become a transaction protocol beyond its cryptocurrency status.

Therefore, as an investor, you always look for ways to make your business easy and convenient. Hence, by investing in Ripple (XRP), every investor would deal with his business more reliably.

Minimizing The Risk in Cryptocurrency Portfolio

Stick To a Reliable Strategy

One of the most important ways of gaining profits through your investments is strategic planning. This comprises buying cryptocurrencies in low values and selling them at higher profitable prices in the market. However, this requires a long-term hold and patience for a better outcome with your investments.

Hence, it is suggested to buy crypto coins in bulk when the prices drop down extremely low. This is possible with cryptocurrency since one cannot predict the market value of any digital coin.

Allocations

As an investor, there comes a lot of confusion when it comes to planning your investments in cryptocurrency. While building a portfolio, it is always better to invest in different coins of different market values. This leads you to the diversity of your cryptocurrency portfolio.

People might have a view that investing all the money in one coin will multiply their investments within a few days. However, this is not the case with the cryptocurrency market. Therefore, it is better to invest in high, moderate, and low-risk coins.

At the end of the day, the investor becomes more confident about his investments. This is because diversity minimizes the risk in your cryptocurrency portfolio. Therefore, build a cryptocurrency profile with a diverse range of coins.

Exchanges

Cryptocurrency exchanges play a huge role in evaluating your growth in the cryptocurrency world. Firstly, the reputation of the exchanges among your community members will help you out to enlist the topmost ones. For this matter, you can use different platforms to research exchanges available near your residence.

Then comes the fee charges for the exchanges to work for us. So, a clever person should analyze all the things including the exchange fees while building a cryptocurrency portfolio. Knowing fees will help with your future transactions, withdrawals, and deposits as a part of your investments.

One Investment at a time

Once a person has decided to invest in cryptocurrency, now it's time to invest your money. It is better to invest a little amount of money as compared to investing a huge amount all at once. For example, if an investor wants to put $800 in a coin. It would be ideal to do small payments for that coin like $50 or $100 per month.

In this way, it enables the investor to see the return of his investments in that specific coin. As there can be ups and downs, so with a little investment at the starting it will not be a huge loss for the investor. Moreover, if the return is bad and prices are dropping, investors can buy more coins at a lower price rather than selling them cheaper.

Nevertheless, A cryptocurrency portfolio is better at outcomes when you have done all the steps to minimize the risks in your investments. Such steps will add value to your coins and will lower the risks of you losing your league in the cryptocurrency world.

Chapter-VIII
Make Money by Mining $1,000 a Month

Try planting your best. You will harvest it later

Cryptocurrencies are the new big thing nowadays. Everyone seems to be intrigued and they want to make money efficiently. Cryptocurrencies are decentralized which means no specific organization controls them. By engaging in cryptocurrency mining, you can gain money without doing any investment. There are few actionable steps that you can take to mine digital currencies like Bitcoin, Litecoin, Ethereum, etc

Usually, the bank authorizes all transactions of the fiat currency all around the world. However, since cryptocurrency is not controlled by a bank, this task is the responsibility of the miners. There is a specific amount of Bitcoin locked in a Bitcoin protocol. It is not possible to generate more than you are supposed to. For this purpose, miners use extremely powerful computers to solve complicated arithmetic questions.

I. The Mining Process

When a miner solves a certain equation, he receives a block reward in the form of digital coins. The mining process validates the transactions on the blockchain and the miner receives the coins in his wallet. The transaction is also recorded on a public database. Moreover, the coins get released in the market as well. Currently, there are about 18 million Bitcoin. As the number increases, the mining process becomes difficult as well.

Furthermore, mining a new block takes only 10 minutes. One block adds 12 Bitcoin to the circulation. So, to start mining you must make sure to have a compatible and reliable wallet. There are a variety of wallets like hardware, desktop, mobile and online. Then, based on the choice of your cryptocurrency, it is required to have mining software. The most important factor is to have a strong internet connection whenever you decide to mine digital coins.

II. Cryptocurrency Mining Rig

In earlier days when Bitcoin was first introduced, miners were able to use a domestic computer and graphic cards to gain coins successfully. However, this doesn't work anymore. It is not possible to mine Bitcoin with an ordinary computer. This will only take a long time and produce a really small amount of coin which won't be profitable. The competition for mining coins has become difficult and there has been a drastic increase in the numbers of people who have become miners today as compared to the past.

To successfully mine Bitcoin or any other crypto coins, special hardware is used. Application-Specific Integrated circuit chips or ASIC is efficient hardware. It uses less energy and mines coins at a fast rate. The speed of ASIC is astonishing. It attempts to solve almost 1012 times to solve a block in a single second. Whatsminer M20S Bitcoin mining machine can generate around $8 a day.

Mining Bitcoin requires a lot of electricity. They emit heat and noise as well. To avoid these issues, you can either hire a mining company or a professional mining center where you can keep your machine. They provide a well-ventilated and cool area and monitor the device around the clock. This way you'll be able to gain profit without having to be bothered by anything.

III. Mining Pools

Another thing that you should know about is that mining on your own is not always fruitful. For this, it is important to join mining pools. This is a cooperation between miners that enables them to work together and share their resources in the mining process. When coins are mined, it gets divided among them according to the resources they provided.

Although, the members of the pool have to pay a specific fee to the main operator. But it is just about 2% of the received coins. This way you can gain coins without putting much effort yourselves. The daily income might be low but it will be steady. In no time, you'll be able to get an adequate number of coins weekly and monthly.

IV. Is it Worth the Hassle?

Many people wonder if mining crypto coins is worthwhile or not. If you ask most miners, they would probably give you a pessimistic answer. Mining Bitcoin is hard however, you should choose to mine other cryptocurrencies as well. This would help you to gain extra income. So, to decide if mining cryptocurrency is worthy and profitable, several aspects need consideration.

After choosing the digital currency, buy the right kind of rig as there are many options available in the market. Operational costs, hash rate, reward, and difficulty are the main factors that determine the level of profitability. You can opt for home mining, cloud mining, or even specialized mining. But home mining is often not profitable, cloud mining possesses certain to rise and specialization is not easily accessible.

Cryptocurrency mining is a business. Therefore, you can expect little to no profit. It is important to have realistic expectations. Over time, this mining process will be more popular and the rates are going to increase too. Moreover, cryptocurrency rates fluctuate continuously. There is no certainty if the amount will increase or decrease. One way is to use online blockchain platforms which are easily accessible and provides you with a substantial profitable income.

V. The Best Available Mining Hardware

- **Alienware Aurora R11 Gaming Desktop**

One of the most excellent mining PC money can buy is Alien Aurora R11. It has an Intel 17-10700KF processor which has 8cores with 16 threads. This provides the chance to multitask efficiently. It also has an NVidia GPU. Moreover, there is space available in case you want to upgrade in the future.

- **Bitmain Antminer S17 Pro**

This mining hardware has some amazing specifications. There are three modes for mining, normal, low power, and turbo. The lower mode prevents any overheating of the chips. The hash rate of this device is 56TH/s. It is the most efficient ASIC miner. The efficiency power is 93.88±10%. Utilizing ASIC is better than other mining rigs as they don't use GPU for mining. This reduces the price and power consumption.

- **Antminer D3**

Antminer D3 is a fast and mid-range miner. The hash rate is 19.3 GH/s. Moreover, the efficiency rate is 93% and it uses 1200W power. It is one of the most considerable miners that miners can look forward to buying and using.

VI. Cryptocurrencies Other than Bitcoin

Bitcoin is the most preferred coin among miners. It has more popularity, market capitalization, and a bigger user base. The world of cryptocurrency progressed greatly after the launch of Bitcoin. But it is somewhat hard to mine profitably. It is incredibly energy-intensive. This has intrigued miners to mine other digital currency.

Nevertheless, other cryptocurrencies are getting attention as well. For example, Ethereum is used to create a decentralized system for people who are inaccessible to traditional financial products. On the other hand, Litecoin cryptocurrency utilizes the Scrypt method. This is a simple arithmetic process as compared to Bitcoin's SHA-256 method. Consequently, as compared to super expensive and power-consuming rigs for Bitcoin, you can mine Litecoins with powerful graphic cards using a laptop or desktop PC.

The mining speed of Litecoin is faster than Bitcoin. It takes 2 minutes to mine Litecoin whereas it takes more than 10 minutes to mine a Bitcoin block. Therefore, the mining process of Litecoin is easier and quicker. It also offers faster transactions and provides a profitable and stable mining process to miners.

VII. The Advantages of Mining Cryptocurrency

Cryptocurrencies are now mainstream. Every day more and more people are realizing its advantages. Authorities banned it in earlier days since they were not in control of it, however, they now have public pressure to legalize it. The blockchain network is secure and no one can track you through any transactions. You can use it to buy or sell coins as preferred. Moreover, many businesses are now accepting these crypto coins as payment.

Moreover, the contribution of hash power by miners to the network makes it less susceptible to any cyber-attacks. Crypto mining also offers complete discretion and user autonomy. It is better to mine digital currency than buying it. Mining is more cost-effective in the long term. The initial costs might be high but subsequent costs are less. If you make the right decisions, mining can turn out to be cheap and scalable.

You might have heard that crypto mining is not great and must be avoided. Whoever says this needs education and awareness regarding how the mining process works. According to a report, miners use renewable energy to power the mining operation. This prevents the wastage of surplus electricity. Developers are constantly in work to find a way for more energy conservation methods. They want to find an alternative to make this process more environmentally and easy as well.

The decisions you make for choosing the kind of cryptocurrency, the hardware, and method play a significant role in the profitability of cryptocurrency. If you make the right and suitable decision, only then you'll be successful in mining coins with efficiency and stability. It is a great idea to take advice from experienced people. So, do not be in a rush, do proper research, make a specific plan, and then carry on with your cryptocurrency mining endeavors.

Chapter-IX
Can You Be a Millionaire by Investing in Cryptocurrency?

Successful investment is about managing risk, not avoiding it

In the previous years, investing money was only limited to stocks, bonds, land properties, or gold items. As the trading changed globally, now investments can be done in cryptocurrency as well. This became possible due to the high surges of cryptocurrency in the world. Altogether, one can see the increasing supply and demand of cryptocurrency nowadays.

Moreover, there are a total of 984 different cryptocurrencies ruling over the world in recent years. All these magical coins have proven to be the most ultimate way of trading and exchange for the investor. The current cryptocurrency market can be seen shooting higher with no looking back at the moment. Therefore, people are looking forward to starting investing in cryptocurrency.

Why Choosing Cryptocurrency for Your Investments

The cryptocurrency was introduced as a digital currency with peer-to-peer network worldwide. The main idea behind digital currency is to simplify the mode of transferring money for goods and services in the coming years. Thus, it is neither regulated by any banking service nor any government authority.

One might have been confused about the fuss of cryptocurrency in the market. If it's not owned by any authority then why people are still interested in cryptocurrency. This is because of the many logical reasons which have attracted investors towards digital currency.

Guaranteed Returns

The most incredible benefit of cryptocurrency should be considered first and foremost in the list. It is none other than the amount of return from the cryptocurrency investments. While looking at the history of cryptocurrency, you can understand why there's so much hype about it. This is only because of the reason that cryptocurrency has secured the top place in the market over a short period.

Due to the increasing value of cryptocurrency in the market, it has immensely increased the stock market of cryptocurrency, especially Bitcoin. For example, your return could be 20% higher in the USA market. In other words, cryptocurrency can make you a millionaire in a short period.

Solely Owned Investments

With the previous investment options, there was the involvement of third parties most of the time. This resulted in commissions and frauds in the investment process. Supposedly, when you keep your money in the bank and you want to invest that money, you will go through different steps to finally start investing them. Likewise, there's a possibility to be restricted by the government rules and regulations.

However, in the cryptocurrency world, it is not the same. Cryptocurrency makes you the only owner of your money. Your money will remain with you forever with no third-party involvement. When you are investing in cryptocurrency, there's no longer concern about any banking fees or regulations. This altogether can make you at the top list of a decentralized economy state.

The Liquidity Value

The next important thing to consider about the investment is the liquidity. You have to ask, how liquid is your investment? Liquidity is related to the growth of your investments in the market. It is concerned with the chances of you selling or buying the investment at a rate that is close to the market value.

Secondly, different tools have been developed to limit the selling or buying of cryptocurrency at a specific price. At the end of the day, your money in the cryptocurrency investment is safe from loss as compared to the other investment options.

THINGS TO KNOW BEFORE INVESTING IN CRYPTOCURRENCY

Volatility

The value of Cryptocurrency changes rapidly with a swing in a very short period. This adds volatility in cryptocurrency investments globally. However, it is suggested to get advice from the stock market expertise to avoid any risks. The volatility can be in the favor of the investor as well. For example, Bitcoin went from $900 to $20,000 within 2017. Nevertheless, all types of investments carry the risk of losing money.

Research Makes It Perfect

On the other hand, a beginner with good research and knowledge about the current trends of cryptocurrency can top the market as well. If you are aware enough about cryptocurrency, it will boost your stocks as well. Stocks and shares of cryptocurrency investments will drive your fortune to a better life.

Be Confident About Your Money

Investing your hard-earned money requires patience throughout the journey. No one became a millionaire overnight. Start an investment with a little chunk of money, especially for cryptocurrency investments. Figure out the different types of cryptocurrencies in the market and make your investments diversified.

There will be a lot of rich schemes available in cryptocurrency but do not trust them at all. It's your money so choose to invest wisely with your research about cryptocurrency. A lot of scams are present in the digital market these days. So, it is always better to do your research and start investing with confidence.

Initial Coin Offerings (ICO)

Initial Coin Offerings (ICOs) work as a fundraiser for a cryptocurrency startup company. It is evolving as a new strategy for cryptocurrency investors. The companies raise money through ICOs. The companies use that money for the developing of blockchain or cryptocurrency-related products. Unlike IPO in share market, there is no government regulation involved in ICO.

Secondly, ICOs give digital tokens rather than giving shares to their clients. For a small business that is an excellent option to invest in cryptocurrency. Initial Coin Offerings save the investors from facing the bankers or other capitalists. This will enable the startup to achieve its objectives as soon as possible.

If you can identify any solid companies issuing ICO, it would be worth considering investing in them. For example, If Elon Musk declares creating a new Cryptocurrency, I will jump onto it straight way. Similarly, I would invest in Mark Zuckerberg's cryptocurrency. I know they have huge customer base, in few years' time, the price of their coins will go up. If you are lucky, you can be a millionaire in no time.

Top Cryptocurrency Stocks in The Market

In recent years, cryptocurrency created a major breakthrough in attracting investments. Investors are keen to put their money into the digital currency. Because of the rising price trend of Bitcoin, almost everyone is talking about investing in cryptocurrency. Due to higher investment return possibilities, crypto stocks are gaining worldwide investors' attention.

At the dawn of cryptocurrency, no one imagined that these magical coins would be leading the investing world. However, many people challenged their luck and invested in cryptocurrency. They became millionaire almost overnight. According to the reports, the top three crypto stocks to kick off your investments are as follows.

Facebook (FB)

An increasing number of investors are supporting the digital currency market. Facebook owner Mark Zuckerberg decided to make his debut in cryptocurrency as well. He has developed Diem as a new cryptocurrency that has replaced an old one named Libra.

Diem is different from the mainstream cryptocurrency in the market. This is because of two main reasons associated with Diem. One is that FB cryptocurrency Diem is a fiat currency and it is regulated by a central authority as well. It is predicted that Facebook will add this currency in its wallet Novi sooner.

As a social media giant, Diem stocks backed by FB will no doubt favor the investors as well. Facebook having a huge user-friendly platform will promote the small business too.

At the moment, the FB owner is waiting for approval from the Swiss Financial Market Supervisory Authority to launch Diem in the market. Hence, FB's step towards cryptocurrency will open a gateway for the new investor to boost up the stock market.

PayPal (PYPL)

The next top-ranked stock for cryptocurrency is PayPal. Being a successful money transfer company on its own, PayPal has done wonders in the cryptocurrency world too. The stocks of PayPal reached their highest rates in October 2020.

PayPal developers modified their investment plans and allowed the users to manage the currency in their own PayPal platform. And this in turn enabled the investors to simply buy, sell and hold their investments by using their all-time favorite application PayPal. This gave a huge breakthrough to PayPal in the cryptocurrency market.

There's also good news for the PayPal users who wish to invest in cryptocurrency. PayPal has planned to integrate cryptocurrency into the mainstream PayPal services. This will enable the users to use cryptocurrency for their goods and services. Ultimately, it will lead to more surges in cryptocurrency investments.

According to the experts, PayPal's initiative towards cryptocurrency will pave the way for investors from all business sectors.

Square (SQ)

The third number on the list of crypto stocks and it is scored by Square (SQ). The company is known for its multipurpose platform regarding payments and exchange. Square came into the spotlight when the company reached up to $28,000 for its Bitcoin stocks.

A very unique feature of Square(SQ) is that the investor can invest in cryptocurrency using the company's Cash App. This new platform generated a revenue of $1.63 billion in the year 2020. It is the only company that is upgrading its team members to introduce more Bitcoin projects in the market.

Being a payment platform, cryptocurrency trading will investors help to produce trillions of revenue globally. Therefore, Square (SQ) is the ultimate player in the cryptocurrency stock market.

After reading the cryptocurrency investment pros and cons, strategies, and options, you can have an image of your money being invested into the world of crypto coins. These coins will surely change your fortune and make you a millionaire within the next few months of your life.

Chapter-X

How the Blockchain Technology Changing the World

Revolution is not a moment; it is a series of events impacting every aspect of lives

The Implementation of Blockchain Technology in the Third World Countries

Land Registration:

While blockchain has proven to be a milestone in the field of technology in progressive and developed countries, it has also undoubtedly proven to be a good fortune by empowering many of the developing countries.

Many countries including India and Honduras are now experimenting to develop blockchain-based land title registries. This will be executed by instilling the decentralized and verification system of blockchain technology that will ensure the security of property rights while simultaneously enhancing transparency in the process to combat any form of corruption and fraud.

This will bring forth a ground-breaking revolution that is much needed especially in third-world countries where rights of land ownership are often a cause of homicide and murder. One such system called ConsenSys has already been developed in Chandigarh city of India to manage land ownership records.

Voter Registration:

Voter registration integrity and election security have been a pressing concern both the government and the public, which is where blockchain technology provides an ideal solution by its system of transparency that retains the privacy of the voters and minimizes election tampering.

This system has been implemented in Sierra Leone on March 7, 2018, when Sierra Leone - the first one to embark on this journey of technology revolution by using this system in Presidential elections. This technology which is created by Leonardo Gammar of Agora allows the voters to vote anonymously and stores these anonymous votes in an immutable ledger. It provides the opportunity to finalize the election result within an hour.

Fake Certificates:

The decentralized, verification system of the blockchain algorithm has been revered worldwide for providing such an excellent and efficient security system and protocol to its users. This distributed ledger system (DLS) of blockchain has prevented many frauds, forgery, and counterfeit many certificates and licenses. A blockchain-based authentication system will have the ability to single out fake diplomas and certificates, thereby preventing any more corruption from society. This certificate, applying the system of smart contract, will help in land rights, will rights, and de-eliminating the fake certificate falsifying the educational background of an individual among many others.

Providing Opportunities To Under Developed Countries

According to global reports, more than half of the population has no access to basic banking services in their areas. This lack of service makes it difficult for them to pay loans, utilities and deal with financial crises. Thus, such people tend to minimize their financial crises by taking shortcuts and dealing with issues later on. Here comes cryptocurrency to simplify the lives of people with poor banking services available.

Digital coins provide easy and secure options to the majority of the population worldwide. Now, third world countries have the luxuries of using the decentralized currency system for their citizens. Various programs and platforms have been developed to facilitate the cryptocurrency market. This adds more value to the investments of cryptocurrency.

According to Money control, it has been estimated that India currently holds Rs. 10, 000 crores in cryptocurrency. Despite the many rumors of a ban or restriction on it the cryptocurrency is thriving and leading the country in a uniquely decentralized direction. It is believed that these famous cryptocurrencies such as CoinSwitch Kuber will pave the path for India to a more revolutionized future.

As a result, it is expanding the audience of cryptocurrency day by day. Their decentralized system has cut down the trading issues across the borders. Whether you are a trader or an investor, you can easily exchange goods freely across the borders now.

Minimizing The Transaction Fees

As per the structure of blockchain, cryptocurrency requires no specific network to function properly. Therefore, this has caused a reduction in the processing fee of cryptocurrency. Dealing with digital currency also does not require any manpower, a proper setup, or any specific Platform. This makes digital trading free from any bills, employees, or extra taxes.

Due to its almost zero costs to send money overseas, more people are showing interest in cryptocurrency. This raises the graphs of digital currency on a large scale. Ultimately, it increases the chances for cryptocurrency to take over the traditional money system in the world.

Transparency Over Transactions

Being a peer-to-peer network, cryptocurrency solely works through its blockchain system. This enables the users to make transactions without any hassle.

The blockchain saves all the data of transactions on automation. This removes every chance of fraud and corruption from cryptocurrency investments. So, the countries that have poor governance structures, can also boost their economy through cryptocurrency.

Cryptocurrency Changing the World Economy

Empowering E-Commerce Sector

Cryptocurrency not only revolutionized trading but also influenced e-commerce in a good way. People are now looking forward to spending online for daily life expenditures. On the other hand, the simple methodology of cryptocurrency has made it easier for the consumer worldwide.

When it comes to small ventures, they have also been facilitated by cryptocurrency. It has minimized the risk of fraud for both the vendors and the customers. This ultimately helps the small business to grow as they can get goods from the market without any regular cash restrictions.

Increases The Exports

Due to low transaction fees and secure money transfers, cryptocurrency is also being used by traders. This increases the exchange of goods and services across borders. Altogether the exports of a country would be uplifted by trading in cryptocurrency.

On the other hand, as digital money is easy to convert into any currency worldwide, it is more convenient for investors. Their low costs, faster transactions, and secure network makes them ideal for cross borders services. Hence, cryptocurrency can increase exports many times more than traditional cash.

Uplifting The Global Remittances

People living in different parts of the world have been using various money transfer options lately. It can be MoneyGram, Western Union, PayPal, Remitly or so on. The most common drawback of all these firms was the high percentage of fees being deducted in each transaction. Secondly, it took days for the money transfer to reach its final destination.

Whereas cryptocurrency money transfer is concerned, it is much faster and more secure than the previously available options. As discussed earlier, it costs very low to send money to various parts of the world. This option of cryptocurrency can also be used to pay for your goods worldwide. Overall, this increases the global remittance which is driven through cryptocurrency usage in the world.

How Blockchain shaping third world Political Environment

The advent of blockchain technology has brought forth many golden opportunities especially to the third world countries by shaping and molding the political environment of the countries and bringing a more positive image. The decentralized system of blockchain serves a unique and important purpose by allowing the political environment to be more democratic in nature, thus preserving the rights of the citizens and allowing them more freedom and control over their money and protecting their voting rights.

This system of transparency has opened a new window towards a world with no government corruption by allowing the citizen to be the watchdogs of their own rights and assets. This system gives permits the citizen to freely live in a state with no panic or anxiety over being watched and continually regulated by the government. As we discussed in the previous sections, the land registry in India and implementation of blockchain to help out Syrian refugees etc. are just a few examples how blockchain has affected the political and societal climate of third world countries.

Hence, the implementation of Blockchain especially in the third world countries will bring forth a more democratic political environment, favored by the citizens.

Chapter-XI
How To Avoid Crypto Scams

The best way to avoid a scam is to prepare for it

How are Crypto Scammers Screwing Common People?

We all are familiar with scams. However, things get even messier when it comes to Bitcoin and cryptocurrencies in general. Bitcoin is known to be an unregulated currency so it is essentially a money bag with a lock on it. And it is expected that only the owner knows the code. However, if by some miracle, someone cracks this code, the owner is at risk of losing all his credit. This is all due to the fact that Bitcoin is a decentralized system with no authority keeping a check on it. Hacking into the blockchain system of Bitcoin is nothing less than a strenuous challenge, however, that has not stopped hackers and cons to give it a shot.

There are different kinds of Bitcoin scams, but these are among the greatest to report. Remain aware.

- MALWARE SCAMS

    Plenty of internet scams have been utilized with malware for a long time. However, because of the existence of fiat currency, it faces a significant threat for cryptocurrencies.

    According to yahoo finance, a software support forum named bleeping computer recently released an alert about cryptocurrency targeting malware in the hopes of preventing consumers from sending crypto coins via purchases.

    This kind of malware scam is known as cryptocurrency clipboard hijackers. According to Lawrence Abraham, tech forensics and developer of bleeping computers, it monitors the Windows clipboard for cryptocurrency addresses. If one is located, it replaces it with the one they command.

- PONZI SCHEME

    Ponzi Bitcoin scam has to be the worst possible mix of terms for finance experts; however, the truth is much worse.

    You will see late night adverts on local cable network or YouTube Ad that they will pay you money if you get someone to sign up on their Bitcoin Scheme. They also shamelessly promote celebrity's photograph to create an impression as if those celebrities endorsed the scheme. This is downright fraud. In South Korea, people have been defrauded millions of dollars through a website called mining max.

In all cases, these platforms are not registered with the stock and exchange commission in USA or any country. However, they offer regular commission for initial deposit and referring others for their services. You should not buy their Ponzi scheme at any time.

The famous case of Ponzi scheme was Bitconnect. To tell you a short story, Bitconnect was formed with the intention of lending Bitconnect coin to earn interest. This scheme was unregistered with any government. Often, the promoter of Bitconnect offered false and misleading information to public.

- **BITCOIN GOLD SCAM**

The possibility of gold through Bitcoin gold captures the eye of the innocent like nothing else. According to CNN, the Bitcoin gold wallet defrauded customers out of three-point two million dollars in the year 2017 by promising to help them claim their Bitcoin gold. The website falsely used links on reputable Bitcoin gold websites to convince investors about giving the Bitcoin gold scam their pirate keys or seeds.

According to CNN, the website administrators which are known as the Bitcoin gold scammers were able to obtain one hundred and seven thousand dollars' worth of Bitcoin gold, seventy-two thousand dollars' worth of Litecoin, thirty thousand dollars' worth of Ethereum, and three million dollars' worth of Bitcoin before the scam was accomplished.

How To Protect Yourself from Crypto Scams?

Before trusting any wallet or swapping a web or app, all users must perform comprehensive research to acknowledge all about its credibility and transactions. Also, it is more likely to be a scam website if the exchange is new to the industry and it explodes causing people to start making headlines in a hurry.

Just as to protect yourself from Malware scams, you need to keep updating your antivirus software from time to time and prevent opening uncertain or suspicious attachments. Besides, prevent downloading or installing any software until you've double-checked that it's secure. Additionally, another red flag on exchanges is that they give a big discount to potential customers entrapping them into being fraud victims.

Moreover, don't deposit money or give away personal details, and don't use an app store as well to get any wallet, before you made your mind up by doing complete research on it. Finally, people should check the certification of an exchange URL to see whether it is genuine or not.

How To Spot a Scam?

Micro-cap investment is much riskier than big-cap investing that leads to the conclusion. Since liquidity is typically low, you may not be able to sell a micro-cap stock fast enough to minimize your losses if anything goes wrong. Earnings are always negative and large gaps may have built up. These businesses are similar to shooting stars, in that they can burn out almost as quickly as they can light up the sky.

Moreover, if you are searching for a microcap stock, start with the EDGAR database, as even the tiniest firms are required to file financial disclosures with the SEC. Also, industries with less than the worth ten million dollars are not expected to register. Although they usually do when they intend to sell their shares to general public. However, the other micro-caps, which share publicly traded shares but are not required to file with the securities and exchange commission.

The examples of these anomalies are, as mentioned, In Reg A offerings, the company raises less than five million dollars in a year. Whereas, in Reg B offerings, the company raises less than one million dollars in a year. This clarifies with all the acknowledgments to spot microcap scams.

Don't fall For Greed or High Returns in Crypto

Let's face it, people want to become overnight Bitcoin millionaire. It's nothing but greed. And, Greed is not good always.

When you are influenced by greed, you won't read the fundamentals of a coin. Rather, you will fall for scammer's promise to become a millionaire just with simple steps or depositing $1,000 to their trading account. I have seen people who rushed to Bitcoin trading without realizing the risk part, lost all of their savings. Sometimes, people feel the peer pressure to make a quick million out of Bitcoin investment as many people became so. You need to understand they started several years ago.

As a result, they believe that investing is the only way to make money through Bitcoin. Unfortunately, they overlook the fact that trading is a distinct practice that necessitates a unique set of skills. They don't realize that not every can become a good trader.

Bitcoin is much more than a quick money scheme; however, it is designed to save you from bankruptcy over time as a result of the shortcomings of the present monetary and financial systems. Additionally, Richard Nixon was the one who unilaterally instituted the new Monterey and financial regime in August, 1971. He voted to terminate the US dollars gold convertibility and, the Jamaica Accords, which were signed in January year 1976, reiterated this framework.

The Pump and Dump Scheme

The pump and dump strategy isn't new, it's been used widely in the financial markets for quite some time. Although the con's concept is straightforward. An individual or a group buys a significant volume of a security or a token that is critical and thinly priced and the price increases as a result.

Moreover, if the asset price rises as the result of the original purchase, the individual who made the purchase will continue to promote the asset mostly through informal media. If more consumers invest, that is more likely to cause the price to rise even higher and people will become enthralled by the promise of even greater profits.

Furthermore, the company behind the original purchases and public relations drive is now able to cash out its holdings at a much higher price range, locking in some significant profits. Also, anyone who enters the market late in the period is more likely to be left with the asset, as there will be no sellers available, which is known as the end of the scheme.

In general, after the original shareholder who started the scheme left the market and the advertisement push fades away, the stocks will drop and anybody with shares or tokens is more likely to suffer significant losses. In nutshell, that's how the pump and dump scheme is briefed.

You can read the famous case study of Bitconnect by googling it.

How To Spot Pump and Dump Scheme?

The simplest way to spot a pump and dump scheme is when an unseen coin unexpectedly increases in value without any justifications. It is apparent in the coins price table. Also, often when you see paid-for news stories about a small-cap coin occurring alongside an increase in social network activity around the specific cryptocurrency initiative that is more likely to indicate a pump. Moreover, one should be cautious if an almost unknown coin with a market capitalization of just a few million dollars unexpectedly emerges on social media platforms.

How To Avoid or Minimize Crypto Risks?

Diversification is maybe the most obvious thing you can do to protect your investments when putting them to work. Also, make sure not to throw all of your crypto eggs in one pot. However, if cryptocurrency working isn't your full-time job and you don't have enough time to constantly study the variety of securities, there are some simpler alternatives for the part-time trader to consider.

Such as, one of them is hedging, even if people do not understand what hedging means, eventually most people have heard the term hedge fund. Hedging in cryptocurrencies has the same purpose as it does in conventional finance that is offsetting future risks with a counterpart fund. It is essentially a scheme of insurance. Besides that, there are a few further simpler and similar alternatives as well, that you can consider.

Conclusion

"Well, I think it is working. There may be other currencies like it that may be even better. But in the meantime, there's a big industry around Bitcoin—People have made fortunes off Bitcoin, some have lost money. It is volatile, but people make money off of volatility too."

-Richard Branson

This quote perfectly summarizes the book.

After reading the eleven chapters, you know the bitcoin and other cryptocurrency fundamentals. Buying and storing cryptocurrency were explained in detail.

Each chapter was carefully written to give you a comprehensive idea of bitcoin taxation, bitcoin mining, and the ecosystem of cryptocurrency.

Also, how cryptocurrency changing the third world countries' economies and eliminating corruption were discussed. Ultimately, this will create demand for cryptocurrencies.

Importantly, you now know how to avoid crypto scams and save your hard-earned money.

Now, you know investing in Bitcoin is volatile in nature. This book doesn't encourage you to go after cryptocurrency investing in full swing.

You have read the book because you want to know about cryptocurrency and make an informed investment decision.

Never invest everything in one cryptocurrency. Be cautious about the investment that you can't afford to lose. The ideal scenario would be to invest only 20% of the total investment portfolio in one currency.

Only invest in a cryptocurrency that you understand and find lucrative for your future wealth.

Now make an informed decision about Bitcoin and other cryptocurrencies.

Feedback!

How'd You Enjoy Reading the Cryptocurrency book?

Let me take this opportunity to 'Thank You' for purchasing and reading this book. I am assuming you enjoyed reading it and got some actionable information out of it. I really hope this book made you knowledgeable about cryptocurrency investing.

My readers are my world. I sacrificed my weekends, weekday nights to create this book. I want to spread the knowledge so that others can benefit.

If you enjoyed reading this book and found some valuable information out of it, I would appreciate your support and hope that you could take a moment to post a review on Amazon. I would love to hear from you, even if you have feedback, as it helps me in ensuring that I improve this book and others in the future.

If you want to write to me, surefinancialfreedom@gmail.com

References

Nakamoto, S., & Bitcoin, A. (2008). A peer-to-peer electronic cash system. Bitcoin.–URL: https://bitcoin.org/bitcoin. pdf, 4.

Ron D., Shamir A. (2013) Quantitative Analysis of the Full Bitcoin Transaction Graph. In: Sadeghi AR. (eds) Financial Cryptography and Data Security. FC 2013. Lecture Notes in Computer Science, vol 7859. Springer, Berlin, Heidelberg. https://doi.org/10.1007/978-3-642-39884-1_2

Aggarwal, V. K., & Marple, T. (2020, December). *Digital currency wars? Us-china competition and economic statecraft.* Retrieved from https://www.globalasia.org/v15no4/feature/digital currency-wars-us-china-competition-and-economic-statecraft_vinod-k-aggarwaltim-marple:

Ølnes, S., Ubacht, J., & Janssen, M. (2017). *Blockchain in government: Benefits and implications of distributed ledger technology for information sharing.* Retrieved from https://www.sciencedirect.com/science/article/abs/pii/S0740624X17303155

Bizonex. (2020, April 30). *Blockchain and crypto: Hype or financial revolution?* Retrieved from Medium: https://medium.com/bizonex/blockchain-and-crypto-hype-or-financial-revolution b5e659540559

Panda, S. K., Elngar, A. A., Balas, V. E., & Kayed, M. (2020). *Bitcoin and Blockchain: History and Current Applications (Internet of Everything (IoE))* (1st ed.). CRC Press. https://doi.org/10.1201/9781003032588

Saunokonoko, M. (2021, January 13). *Man who forgot password on brink of losing $300m Bitcoin fortune.* Breaking Australian and World News Headlines - 9News. Retrieved from https://www.9news.com.au/technology/us-man-has-just-2-password-attempts-left-or-will lose-300-million-bitcoin-fortune/fa9c5c1b-23bc-4107-a6f1-a3e288747027

Ponciano, J. (2021, April 18). *Crypto Flash Crash Wiped Out $300 Billion In Less Than 24 Hours Spurring Massive Bitcoin Liquidations.* Retrieved from Forbes. https://www.forbes.com/sites/jonathanponciano/2021/04/18/crypto-flash-crash-wipedout 300-billion-in-less-than-24-hours-spurring-massive-bitcoin-liquidations/?sh=7fd3d81d2c89

Neuburger, J. (2017, April 20). *Arizona Passes Groundbreaking Blockchain and Smart Contract Law State Blockchain Laws on the Rise.* The National Law Review. https://www.natlawreview.com/article/arizona-passes-groundbreaking-blockchain-and smart-contract-law-state-blockchain

Bambrough, B. (2020, March 19). *Here's What Caused Bitcoin's 'Extreme' Price Plunge.* Forbes. https://www.forbes.com/sites/billybambrough/2020/03/19/major-bitcoin-exchange bitmex-has-a-serious-problem/?sh=1513fb344f7d

National Institute of Standards and Technology. (2020). *Hash Functions.* Retrieved from https://csrc.nist.gov/Projects/Hash-Functions

www.ingramcontent.com/pod-product-compliance
Lightning Source LLC
Chambersburg PA
CBHW070816220526
45466CB00002B/680